Sicily: whose victory?

S0-BRG-456

Sicily:

whose victory?
Martin Blumenson

Editor-in-Chief: Barrie Pitt
Art Director: Peter Dunbar

Military Consultant: Sir Basil Liddell Hart
Picture Editor: Robert Hunt

Executive Editor: David Mason
Designer: Sarah Kingham
Cover: Denis Piper
Research Assistant: Yvonne Marsh
Cartographer: Richard Natkiel
Special Drawings: John Batchelor

Ballantine Books Inc.
101 Fifth Avenue, New York, NY 10003

Contents

The first assault on Europe

Introduction by Captain Sir Basil Liddell Hart

The invasion of Sicily in July 1943 signalised the Allies' re-entry into Europe, and was the first step in their liberation of the European Continent from Hitler's grip. It came three years after his conquest of the West in 1940, the fall of France, and the expulsion of the British.

In retrospect, the Allied invasion of Sicily looks a certain success, and in the event that great Italian island was completely cleared – of German and Italian troops – in five and a half weeks. Actually, however, it was a hazardous leap, and hedged with uncertainties.

Although the Allied landing in North-West Africa – French North Africa – the previous November had initially met considerable opposition, from French troops, the landing in Sicily was the first, apart from sea-borne raids, when the Allies had to face and overcome actual enemy forces. The successful outcome was greatly helped by the cumulative effect of mistakes and dissensions on the opposing side, among the enemy's top leaders. One was Mussolini's jealous fear of his German allies, and reluctance to let them take a leading part in the defence of Italian territory. Another was Hitler's belief, contrary to Mussolini's, that Sicily would not be the Western Allies' next objective – a mistaken belief that was fostered by the British ruse planted by the 'deception plan'. The third, and most important of all, was the conjoint pride of Mussolini and Hitler in striving to maintain their hold on North Africa too long – a decision basically prompted by the desire to 'save face' without due regard to the strategic consequences.

That was the more surprising on Hitler's part, for he and his General Staff had always been hesitant about embarking on oversea expeditions in reach of British seapower, and had only sent a small German force (under Rommel) to stave off an Italian collapse in February 1941, and had subsequently abstained from sending Rommel sufficient reinforcements to follow up his remarkable string of victories over the British. Yet in the last phase of the North African campaign Hitler and his staff, in accord with Mussolini, had poured so many troops across the sea, into Tunisia, as to sacrifice the chances of defending Europe.

If it had not been for the fact that these forces, amounting to nearly quarter of a million troops, were trapped in Tunisia with their backs to the sea, they could have provided a very strong defence of Sicily – and the Allied chances of successful invasion would have been dim. Even as it was, the Italian troops there mustered nearly two thousand – but their morale was low by the time the invaders came, and most of the best Italian troops had been lost in Africa. The main burden of Sicily's defence was carried by the fraction of German troops which had been sent there as a stiffening, a relatively small number that was raised to about sixty thousand by the time that the end came, and it was due mainly to their tenacity that this was delayed several weeks longer than seemed likely after the catastrophic collapse in the campaign's opening days.

It would be difficult to find anyone with such outstanding qualifications for writing the story of the Sicilian campaign as Martin Blumenson. For the last decade and more he has made a prolonged and profound study of amphibious operations. After showing his quality in dealing with the history of the Korean campaign in the early 1950s, he was entrusted with the U.S. Army's official history of the second stage of the Normandy campaign, the volume entitled *Breakout and Pursuit*, and subsequently produced an illuminating book of his own on that subject *The Duel for France*. Since then he has turned his attention largely to the campaigns in the Mediterranean sphere, and written important books on *Anzio* and *Kasserine Pass*. He has shown in a remarkable way how the thoroughness of the official historian can be blended with vividness.

He opens with a gripping chapter on the mishaps of the preliminary airborne landing, and then turns to an able examination of 'Allied Strategy' and how it led to the decision to invade Europe by way of Sicily – instead of by way of Sardinia and Corsica – as the American and some of the British planners originally preferred. The third chapter depicts 'The Axis Situation'. The fourth, a longer one, describes and analyses the seaborne landings, while the fifth deals with 'The Axis Reaction'. Together, these illuminatingly bring out the hazards, and chanciness, of the invasion. The next returns to the problems and troubles of the airborne side of the operation, while the seventh focuses on the crack that came in the Axis alliance. Chapter 8 then traces the development of the invasion, particularly the American drive by Patton's Seventh Army into the west of the island. It is followed by chapters on the German talk-over, Allied changes of plan, and Mussolini's downfall.

Then come a chapter on the Etna line, and the Germans' very stiff resistance there as they withdrew into the north-east corner of Sicily, and a lengthy chapter 13 on 'The Evacuation'. A short 'aside' follows about 'The Slapping Incident' which jeopardised Patton's career. The final chapter, 15, is a good summary of the campaign and discussion of the question of whether it is to be regarded as 'Victory or Defeat?' Strategically, it was an Allied victory, but tactically, the enemy did so well in extremely adverse circumstances, and put up such a prolonged resistance after the initial collapse that, in the author's judgement, the 'moral victory' rested with them.

Martin Blumenson's book is a remarkably clear account of a complex campaign, a key episode of the war. It deals in a very well-balanced way with the issues on which American and British views differed. He does infer, however, that the protraction of the campaign, and its momentous consequences in drawing the Allies into a much more prolonged campaign in Italy, was due largely to defective planning by the British High Command.

The beginning

The sky was clear with the pale blue colour characteristic of the heavens over North Africa in the summertime, but the sun burned like molten steel, and the heat was oppressive on the airfields where heavy and awkward transport planes, some tied to sleek gliders, stood lined up and passive, receiving the attention of perspiring crews who were running last-minute checks.

Nearby in the blessed shade offered by occasional groves of trees or walls of buildings, soldiers rolled bundles of equipment, cleaned and inspected their weapons. Groups clustered around lieutenants and received final briefings. Each man wore a white armband showing a small American or British flag pinned to his right sleeve for identification. There was little horseplay. They watched as trucks moved out on the fields late in the afternoon and as troops loaded gliders and placed equipment in para-racks.

As evening approached, British airborne soldiers, heavily burdened with individual equipment and arms, filed out on the fields and clambered into the gliders. Airplane pilots started

their engines. A quarter of an hour before seven o'clock, simultaneously from several airfields, the first of 109 American C-47's and 35 British Albemarles began to lumber down the runways, gather speed, and rise into the air, each plane towing a Waco or Horsa glider filled with the British airborne troops.

Seven planes and gliders failed to clear the North African coast for one reason or another and turned back. The others made rendezvous over the Kuriate islands and headed for Malta. The sun was setting as the planes neared Malta, but the signal beacon was visible to all pilots except a few at the rear of the column.

As dusk settled over the Mediterranean, deepening the colour of the sea, the wind rose, raising angry flecks of white foam on the water, and a gale began to blow, driving the planes off course, shaking the aircraft and tossing the gliders. One tow rope snapped, and a glider dropped into the Mediterranean.

The pilots fought to keep in position but the formations loosened. Some squadrons were pushed well to the east

Armstrong-Whitworth Albemarle II Glider tug
Engines: Two Bristol Hercules XI, 1,590 hp *Armament:* Two Vickers K guns
Maximum speed: 265 mph at 10,500 mph *Ceiling:* 18,000 feet *Range:* 1,300 miles
Weight loaded: 22,600 lbs *Span:* 77 feet *Length:* 59 feet 11 inches

of the prescribed route, others at the tail were driven forward, overrunning units in the vanguard. Two pilots lost their way over the water and turned south, back to North Africa. A third accidentally released the glider he was towing, and it fell into the sea.

The others, 133 planes and gliders in all, reached Cape Passero, the check point at the southeastern tip of Sicily. The pilots could barely distinguish the dark land mass that was hardly deeper in hue than the inky sea. Two were unable to orient themselves to the ground and flew back to North Africa.

The rest, by now badly mixed, turned north from Cape Passero, then bore northeastward, the pilots searching anxiously for the glider release point off the eastern coast and just south of Syracuse, but the wind was buffeting them. The designated zigzag course they tried to follow threw most of

them entirely off course. As darkness enveloped Sicily, most of the transport pilots were unable to identify the proper release point. About 25 headed back to Africa. The remainder, about 115, released their towed craft.

The gliders set free carried about 1,200 men. This should have been all right, for those who had planned the operation expected accidents to occur, and a total of 1,200, even 1,000, soldiers on the target area would be sufficient to carry out the assigned mission. But of the 115 gliders cut loose somewhere near the release point, more than half dropped into the sea; no more than 54 gliders landed in Sicily, and of these, only 12 were on or near the correct landing zones. Most of the men who were deposited in the water were lost by drownin' ; many of those in the gliders that came to earth were injured in the landings. Some of those who escaped the hazards of coming to

11

The reality: landing, miles from the target, in Sicily

ground in a strange country during the hours of darkness blundered into enemy units and were killed, wounded, or captured.

As a result, instead of at least 1,000 men as had been hoped, only a handful of British airborne troops, less than 100, managed to come to ground safely near the designated landing place; but they assembled, took compass bearings, then set out in the dark and early hours of 10th July 1943 towards their objective, a bridge named Ponte Grande just south of Syracuse.

Two hours after the British airborne troops started to leave the airfields in North Africa, as the sun was setting, the first of 222 C-47's filled with 3,400 American paratroopers rose into the evening sky. The wind was blowing about 30 mph, and from the outset

aerial groups lost cohesion; a quarter moon had appeared, but it gave the pilots little visibility. Their night formation lights were dim and helped but little to promote visual contact among the planes, and flying low over the Mediterranean, just above the water, the pilots found their windshields obscured by salt spray tossed from the heaving sea. Inexperienced in night flying, they straggled, lost their bearings, missed check points, and approached Sicily from all points of the compass. Two pilots gave up and returned to Africa with their paratroopers. A third crashed into the sea.

Only a few pilots were lucky enough to follow the planned route and to reach and recognize the check points at Linoso, Malta, and the southeastern coast of Sicily – yet even they

The morning after: American paratroopers outside Gela

discovered that the final features were obscured by haze, dust, and smoke. The mouth of the Acate river and the Biviere Pond, so clear on the maps, could hardly be seen, let alone identified. As the pilots struggled to avoid colliding in the gale and darkness, as they worked to solve the problem of orientation, anti-aircraft shells arose from Gala, Ponte Olivo, Niscemi – eight planes would be shot down after they released their paratroopers. The few formations that were maintaining a precarious structure fell entirely apart.

Now the major task of the pilots changed. No longer were they concerned about releasing the paratroopers over their correct drop zones; they were feverish in their efforts to have their planes over any ground at all, solid earth, when the men jumped. For falling into the sea meant swift death by drowning.

As a consequence, the paratroopers were dispersed to the four winds. Several hundred men of one battalion came to earth relatively intact, but they were 25 miles from their designated drop zone, only parts of three companies landed near the target. The rest were scattered over southeastern Sicily.

Instead of the sizable force that the planners hoped would be in possession of the high ground named Piano Lupo, selected because of its important road intersection, less than 200 men were occupying the objective at daylight on 10th July.

The Allied strategy

The decision to invade Sicily was a compromise reached only after considerable Anglo-American discussion, debate, and argument over the best way to defeat the European Axis powers of Germany and Italy. The agreement was not entirely satisfactory to either Allied partner – but diverse national interests made better, fuller accord impossible. The Allies were working under terms of a 'Europe First' strategy – which meant conducting limited and defensive action against Japan until victory was won in Europe; but how to gain triumph in the prime operational area was a matter of dispute.

The American strategy was to seek a showdown with Germany. To that end, the American military leaders wished to build up large forces in the United Kingdom, cross the English Channel and invade northwest Europe, then confront the bulk of the enemy forces along the most direct routes to the German homeland. But this course of action depended on a massive build-up of resources in Britain, thus imposing a delay of at least a year – perhaps longer – before a cross-Channel invasion could get under way.

In order to commit American troops into battle more quickly in the European arena, to help the British forces under extreme Axis pressure in Egypt, and to divert Axis forces from the Russian front, the Americans agreed to an Allied invasion of French northwest Africa. But they then found that the landings in North Africa in November 1942, and the subsequent campaign which had been expected to be over quickly, attracted so considerable an amount of Allied resources as to jeopardize the preparations for a cross-Channel operation in 1943. This greatly disturbed the Americans. The British were less concerned. Foreseeing the eventual expulsion of Axis forces from all of North Africa, they looked ahead to exploiting that victory by continuing operations in the Mediterranean area, specifically

by invading Sicily, Sardinia, the mainland of Italy, or southern France. They hoped also that military action in the eastern Mediterranean region would induce Turkey to enter the war on the Allied side.

For the British were developing what would later be called a peripheral strategy – stretching the Axis forces along the whole periphery of occupied Europe by threatening to invade the Channel coast and by nibbling away at the southern approaches to the continent. Primarily, they wished to eliminate Italy from the war, thereby isolating and weakening the Germans, making them more vulnerable to eventual defeat by the cross-Channel invasion which they saw as the climactic event of the war – landings that must be successful beyond any shadow of doubt.

In contrast, the Americans by the end of 1942 were proposing a strategy of three basic elements: a build-up in the United Kingdom for a cross-Channel invasion in 1943; a great air offensive against Germany from bases in Britain, North Africa, and the Middle East; and increased air bombardment of Italy as the means to destroy Italian morale and eliminate that nation from the war. They had no desire to expand or even to continue the war in the Mediterranean area; they wanted instead to initiate direct action against Germany by launching a powerful thrust across the Channel as soon as possible.

The divergence of Allied strategic thought led to a high-level conference in January 1943. President Roosevelt and Prime Minister Churchill, together with their military advisers, met in Casablanca, Morocco, in order to determine what to do once the African campaign came to a close. How should the considerable forces in North Africa then be employed to keep them for remaining idle? Where should the Allies strike next?

The American Joint Chiefs of Staff, led by General George C. Marshall, were apprehensive that the British would insist on invading Sardinia; for the Americans preferred to shift resources from the Mediterranean immediately to the United Kingdom for a cross-Channel endeavour. Ironically the British Chiefs of Staff, led by

General Sir Alan Brooke, were apprehensive that the Americans would insist on invading Sardinia; for the British preferred to seize Sicily, which, they believed, would knock Italy out of the war and compel the Germans to stretch their forces in order to cover occupation and coastal defence duties then being carried out by the Italians.

Figuring that the duration of the North African campaign, longer than anticipated, was making a cross-Channel effort in 1943 manifestly impossible, Marshall acquiesced in an invasion of Sicily. But what then, he asked. 'Was an operation against Sicily merely a means toward an end, or an end in itself? Is it to be part of an integrated plan to win the war or simply taking advantage of an opportunity?'

No answer could be given, for the partners were divided in their methods. The Americans had, as Churchill remarked, an 'undue liking for logical clear-cut decisions,' while the British were inclined toward an opportunist approach to strategy. Nothing more, therefore, was decided than to invade Sicily after completion of the North African campaign – in order to use the large number of troops available in North Africa and in the hope of eliminating Italy from the war, thereby forcing Germany to assume responsibility for Italian commitments.

To carry out the invasion of Sicily, the Combined Chiefs of Staff – the American and British chiefs sitting together – named General Dwight D. Eisenhower, the Supreme Allied Commander in the Mediterranean area, to be the overall commander. Under him, General Sir Harold R. L. G. Alexander was to head the ground forces, Admiral Sir Andrew B. Cunningham the naval forces, and Air Chief Marshal Sir Arthur Tedder the air forces.

But whether the campaign of Sicily would be the last Mediterranean venture or the opening of an enlarged Mediterranean effort could not be determined. The Americans hoped to avoid becoming involved in 'interminable operations in the Mediterranean', while the British found it 'impossible to say exactly where we should stop'.

Four months later, in May, the

Alexander, the land commander

Allied leaders met in Washington, DC, and again at a formal conference tried to iron out their differences. The major question they sought to answer was what to do after they conquered Sicily – for the North African campaign had now come to a successful close, and the Allies possessed the entire southern shore of the Mediterranean. Now they looked to Sicily and beyond. Whether the Sicily campaign produced the collapse of Italy as the Allies hoped, or whether it failed to do so, how should the course of the war be shaped?

The alternatives seemed clear. The Americans argued for a cross-Channel operation, the British for continuing to maintain the offensive momentum and pressure in the Mediterranean area.

Specifically in the Mediterranean, the Allies could move from Sicily into any one of several places, but each had disadvantages. Southern France was profitable only if undertaken in conjunction with a cross-Channel invasion; Sardinia and Corsica could hardly bring Italy to collapse if the conquest of Sicily had not already

done so, and if Italy indeed collapsed as a result of the loss of Sicily, Sardinia and Corsica would probably fall of their own weight. The Italian mainland was inhospitable ground, posing problems of internal security and a large civil affairs commitment, and led only to the formidable barrier of the Alps; the Balkans had even less inviting terrain for mechanized military forces, such as those of the Allies.

Eisenhower's planners looked toward the seizure of Sardinia and Corsica for additional airfields to cover amphibious operations launched near Genoa or Rome, while Eisenhower himself favoured invading the Italian mainland immediately upon the conclusion of the Sicily campaign, unless this interfered with preparations for a cross-Channel attack. The British military chiefs, having narrowed their focus on post-Sicily operations, recommended a descent on the Italian 'toe', followed by an invasion in the 'heel', and finally an advance up the 'boot'. This meant relegating a cross-Channel endeavour to the indefinite future.

The Americans disliked putting off

Cunningham, the naval commander   **Tedder, the air commander**

the cross-Channel attack. They also felt that entering Italy would lead the Allies to commit increasing amounts of men and material into what would soon become a major campaign, located in what could be only a secondary theatre.

The Allied partners then agreed that they would consider all operations beyond Sicily only in terms of whether they facilitated and expedited the cross-Channel invasion of north western Europe. And finally, on this basis, the Americans accepted the elimination of Italy from the war as a prerequisite for re-entry into the north-western portion of the continent; although they insisted that Mediterranean operations in general be restricted in scope and in the numbers of troops employed.

From there, the Allies proceeded to a compromise. They decided to launch a cross-Channel attack in May 1944, meanwhile attempting to eliminate Italy from the war by using the resources available in the Mediterranean theatre, less seven divisions to be transferred to England by November 1943.

But how specifically to knock Italy out of the war and where to go subsequent to Sicily could not be resolved. The best that the Combined Chiefs of Staff could do was to order Eisenhower to plan to exploit the conquest of Sicily as would best, in his opinion, 'eliminate Italy from the war' and 'contain the maximum number ˙of German forces.'

This was far from firm guidance. In an attempt to find a better basis for post-Sicily operations, Churchill, accompanied by Marshall and Brooke, flew to Algiers upon the completion of the Washington conference and there consulted with Eisenhower.

The Supreme Allied Commander was inclined to go from Sicily into the Italian mainland by way of Calabria – that is, across the Strait of Messina – but when Marshall suggested Sardinia and Corsica as appropriate alternative targets, the conferees came to a preliminary decision. Eisenhower would set up two separate planning headquarters, one to prepare an invasion of Sardinia and Corsica, the other to make ready an invasion of the Italian mainland. After the Allies actually invaded Sicily and came face to face with the strength – or the weakness – of the opposition would the final decision be made. Only then and in the light of the criteria established by the Combined Chiefs – eliminate Italy from the war and contain the maximum number of German troops – Eisenhower would recommend the operation or operations he deemed best and the Combined Chiefs would make the choice.

Thus, in the final analysis, the future Allied strategy would depend in large measure on whether the enemy collapsed entirely or resisted fiercely in Sicily.

Ninety miles from Cape Bon, Tunisia, a scant two miles off Calabria on the Italian mainland, roughly the size of Vermont and slightly larger than Wales, Sicily has had strategic importance since the days of antiquity. A stepping stone for Roman, Carthaginian, Moorish, Viking and Norman invaders, Sicily had been transformed by the 1940s – at least in Mussolini's view – into a gigantic, stationary aircraft carrier. Fleets of Italian and German aircraft operating from Sicilian airfields had forced the British to abandon their traditional maritime route between Gibraltar and Alexandria, and only Malta, 120 miles away – beleaguered, bombed, and virtually isolated – still flew the Union Jack. A successful invasion of Sicily would first require a substantial reduction of the Axis air strength based on the island.

A triangular isle called Trinacria by the Greeks, Sicily is rugged and mountainous. The Caronie Mountains in the northeast are the highest, and are topped by Mount Etna, which stands on a base 20 miles in diameter and rises 10,000 feet. The entire northern coast consists of steep and precipitous cliffs facing the sea, and the only sizable area of flat land on the island is around Catania, and there, as well as on the narrow coastal plain along the eastern and southern shores, was where the airfields were located – 19 in all, plus ten landing strips, none more than 15 miles from the shore. They would be an important target for the Allied invaders.

Along the coastal area the roads are good, but in the interior they are poorly surfaced and narrow, with sharp curves and steep grades, for the towns and small cities – established in mediaeval times or earlier – occupy hilltops for defence; and the winding approaches to them, as well as their narrow streets, were designed for pedestrians and mule carts. Most of the 4,000,000 Sicilians lived in these cities and towns.

The shoreline has numerous beaches of sand and shingle and several major ports – Messina near the northeastern tip of the island, Catania and Syracuse on the eastern face, and Palermo, the largest city, near the western side. Messina, the largest port and the terminus of the ferry service from the mainland, was clearly the prime strategic objective, for its swift capture would seal off the defenders of Sicily and block their reinforcement or escape. Yet the heavy fortifications known to exist along the Strait of Messina ruled out a direct blow there, and similar defences ringed Syracuse, the naval base of Augusta, and Palermo.

The Allies would have to come ashore along the unfortified stretches of coastline. But because the technique of unloading supplies across the beaches was still rudimentary and unproved, they wanted to capture at least one port at once, more if possible. Also influencing the selection of landing sites was the range of Allied aircraft, for the distance from bases on Malta and North Africa precluded adequate fighter protection for amphibious assaults at several otherwise favourable beaches.

The Combined Chiefs had contemplated two task forces for the invasion of Sicily, one British, the other American, and to command the British ground forces, Eisenhower named General Sir Bernard L. Montgomery, the Eighth Army commander, who had driven Field-Marshal Erwin Rommel's Italo-German army westward 1,500 miles from Egypt across Libya to Tunisia, but who had failed to trap Rommel in the process. To lead the American forces, Eisenhower chose Major-General George S. Patton, Jr, who had commanded the Western Task Force in the invasion of North Africa, later the II Corps in Tunisia, and would head the Seventh

Army in Sicily.

More contrasting commanders were hard to imagine. Montgomery belonged to the 'tidy' school of thought and was meticulous and cautious; Patton was of the 'rough and ready' variety, dashing and flamboyant.

Immediately above them was Alexander, who had commanded British forces in Burma, then the Middle East, and who had served as Allied army group commander in Tunisia. His planning staff was called Force 141, named from the number of the room in the St George's Hotel in Algiers, where American and British officers had originally met to plan the invasion of Sicily. This staff would become the headquarters of the 15th Army Group, which would be Alexander's instrument for directing the ground warfare on the island.

The Combined Chiefs of Staff suggested an invasion by means of two simultaneous assaults, one near Palermo, the other near Catania. This would give the Allies two of the major ports and ready access to most of the airfields; it also implied a subsequent campaign of two drives converging on Messina, one along the northern shore, the other along the eastern

21

shore. But this concept had several disadvantages – the troops and shipping required for the two landings would be far greater than those needed for a single, concentrated attack; and two widely separated invasion forces could not be mutually supporting; that is, a concerted enemy effort against one landing might drive it into the sea while the other landing force was unable to help.

Alexander looked into the possibility of landing both Montgomery's and Patton's troops in a concentrated assault against the southeastern corner of Sicily, but his staff believed that the ports of Catania, Syracuse, and Augusta, even if immediately captured, would be inadequate to support all the Allied forces required for the operation. Instead, seeking port facilities and the elimination of most of the enemy airfields, the planners recommended two simultaneous assaults, one by the Americans in the western part of Sicily, the other by the British in the southeast, both coming ashore over wide expanses of beach in order to avoid presenting tempting targets to enemy aircraft and artillery. This generally followed the Combined Chiefs of Staff concept, and Alexander issued a preliminary and tentative outline plan along these ines in February.

Montgomery objected. He disliked having his army trying to come ashore while dispersed around the southeastern tip of Sicily along the considerable distance – roughly 100 miles - from Gela to Catania. The troops, he said, would be so stretched as to be vulnerable to counter action. Why not, he suggested, forget the landings at Gela and Licata on the southern coast and, instead, keep the army strong and united on the eastern face? This would mean letting some airfields go, but it was well worth foregoing the prospect of early capture of some airfields, in his opinion, in favour of a strengthened and amphibious assault.

Cunningham and Tedder were outraged. Concentrated landings, Tedder said, would 'gravely affect the whole air situation in the southeast corner of Sicily' and 'seriously increase the risk of loss of the big ships involved in certain of these assaults'. He felt that air superiority was vital to secure adequate ports, and that while he expected to take preliminary aerial action against the enemy air forces, the only sure way to weaken air opposition was to capture the airfields. Agreeing with Tedder, Cunningham preferred widely dispersed landing forces instead of more vulnerable concentrated forces going against the most strongly defended part of the island.

Accepting these objections but also sensitive to Montgomery's viewpoint, Alexander reached into the American forces. He took an American division and put it into the British sector – under Montgomery's control – to execute the Gela and Licata landings, thus permitting Montgomery to keep his other forces concentrated. To compensate for depriving Patton of a division and thereby weakening the American task force, Alexander proposed that the Americans land several days later, after the British were well ashore.

Patton demurred. The same arguments, he said, applied to his landings near Palermo. If an American division were diverted to action in the British sector, he would be unable to take several airfields that would then interfere with his own assault. His viewpoint was valid but disregarded.

Despite widespread dissatisfaction on all sides, Eisenhower accepted Alexander's new plan because of, he said, 'the obvious fact that initial success in the southeast is vital to the whole project.'

Then the British received another division and the necessary shipping to strengthen Montgomery's assault, and Alexander returned the American division to Patton; but he retained the feature of staggered landings, with the British to go first.

Nobody was happy.

Toward the end of April, Montomery sent Alexander a message and raised the issues again. 'Planning so far', he wrote, 'has been based on the assumption that the opposition will be slight and that Sicily will be captured rather easily. Never was there a greater error. The Germans and also the Italians are fighting desperately now in Tunisia and will do so in Italy.'

He still wanted to confine the British landings to a smaller space along the coastline in order to strengthen his assault. Specifically, he advocated that British landings be restricted to the Gulf of Noto south of Syracuse and to both sides of the Pachino peninsula on the southeastern tip. These beaches were within range of supporting fighter aircraft based on Malta and from there, he could capture the port of Syracuse rapidly, then extend northward to take Augusta and Catania, and eventually drive to Messina. Thus, concentrated landings could be easily developed to seize the required ports.

'What about the airfields?' Cunningham and Tedder asked. They pointed to the airfields near Gela and Comiso which were overlooked by Montgomery's plan; planes from these airfields, they said, could raise havoc with the landing forces.

To resolve the issues, Eisenhower called a conference of the principals at Algiers on 29th April, when an officer representing Montgomery came up with what looked like a new idea. Why not have American and British forces assault the southeastern corner together, the British coming ashore along the Gulf of Noto, the Americans landing on both sides of the Pachino peninsula?

Much of Sicily's strategic value derived from its many airfields. *Above:* An Me 110 over the coast. *Below:* An He 111 being refuelled by an Italian ground crew

The alternative routes for the invasion of the 'Soft Underbelly of Europe'

Cunningham protested. Amphibious techniques, he said, required dispersed forces in landings and the immediate seizure of all enemy airfields in order to protect the ships lying off the beaches – and Tedder supported him.

Thus no immediate decision was forthcoming, and Eisenhower called another meeting on 2nd May. Alexander was unable to attend, but Montgomery appeared in person, talked persuasively, argued interminably, and became tiresome, even following Major General W. Bedell Smith, Eisenhower's chief of staff, into the men's room and while they stood at adjacent urinals continued to explain that a concentrated assault would be so strong as to preclude defeat. War is an engrossing subject.

In the end, Montgomery had his way and on the following day Eisenhower made the decision. The invasion of Sicily would be a concentrated thrust limited to the southeastern part of the island, with no independent American assault near the western corner. Nor would there be staggered assaults. In a single simultaneous movement, the Americans would land along the Gulf of Gela from Licata to the Pachino peninsula; the British would come ashore on the eastern coast from the Pachino peninsula almost to Syracuse.

This rejected the belief of the Combined Chiefs of Staff that it was necessary to take major ports and airfields quickly. The Americans would have no major harbour at all along their stretch of coastline, and would have to rely for their supplies on beach unloading operations; furthermore, there would be no immediate move to take important clusters of airfields in the southwest and around Catania. And finally, the subsequent campaign would have to be improvised once the landing forces were ashore.

Tedder and Cunningham remained disturbed – so upset that Eisenhower looked for some way to overcome their objections and remove their dissatisfaction; he found it in the island of Pantelleria. If he could take Pantelleria in what he called a laboratory experiment that would require the investment of relatively few resources, he might provide an asset that would strengthen the invasion plan.

The Axis situation

Pantelleria is five by eight miles in dimension and rugged, with sheer cliffs rising out of the sea. About 120 miles southwest of Palermo, the same distance as British-held Malta from Catania, it had a civilian population of 12,000 people, a military garrison of 12,000 troops, a competent commander and an airfield that could handle about 80 single-engine aircraft. Underground hangars hewn from solid rock provided repair shops impervious to bombardment and the core of the defence was a force of five Italian infantry battalions, most of them untested in battle, supported by anti-aircraft batteries manned by reservists.

When Eisenhower decided to make a single concentrated invasion of Sicily around the southeastern corner, he determined to seize Pantelleria first. Pantelleria in Allied hands would give many advantages – it would remove the serious threat that Italian planes there posed against the Allied landings in Sicily, deny the island as a refuelling base for Italian and German surface craft and submarines, eliminate Axis radio direction finders and shipwatching stations, provide the Allies with excellent navigational aid stations and a superb air-sea rescue base, and, most of all, make it possible to render better air cover for the American landings and, thereby, more opposition to the enemy planes operating from Sicilian airfields that would not be immediately seized.

Eisenhower wanted to take Pantelleria by means of an operation that would be, he said, 'a sort of laboratory experiment to determine the effect of concentrated heavy bombing on a defended coastline.' He directed Tedder 'to concentrate everything' – all his available bombers – and to blast the island repeatedly to the point where the damage to garrison, equipment, and morale would be 'so serious as to make the landing a rather simple affair.' The British 1st Infantry Division was to make that landing and seize and occupy not only Pantelleria but also the smaller nearby islands of Lampedusa, Linosa, and Lampione.

The idea was daring, for Fascist propaganda proclaimed Pantelleria to be an impregnable fortress. And so it appeared.

But despite Fascist claims, increasingly heavier bombardments from the air and a strong naval shelling soon reduced Pantelleria to shambles. Italian casualties were few, but damage to housing, roads, and communications was extensive and severe and by 1st June the port was in ruins, the town destroyed, the electric plant knocked out. Shortages of water, ammunition, and suppplies, together with the virtually incessant explosions, were beginning to affect morale.

Still the bombing continued. During the first ten days of June, more than 3,500 planes dropped almost 5,000 tons of bombs on Pantelleria, leaflets urging surrender, and finally a surrender ultimatum. The island commander, Admiral Gino Pavasi, had a single radio station still operating by this time, and he informed Rome that he was not even going to bother replying to the Allied ultimatum. A few days later he told Rome that another ultimatum arrived, and that again he would refuse even to acknowledge it. 'Despite everything,' Pavasi assured Rome, 'Pantelleria will continue to resist.'

Successive messages told of Pantelleria's crumbling endurance, but Pavasi made no mention of surrender.

On the morning of 11th June, in good weather, in a calm sea, with the sky clear except for a few low-hanging clouds, the Allied invasion fleet bearing the British 1st Division arrived about eight miles off the harbour entrance to the port of Pantelleria. There the ships halted, anchored, and lowered landing craft, though from their positions Pantelleria was hardly visible; it was cloaked in a haze and dust raised by an Allied air bombardment an hour or so earlier.

Pavasi reported to Rome that morning that Allied bombers had plunged Pantelleria into 'a hurricane of fire and smoke,' adding the ominous news that 'the situation is desperate, all possibilities of effective resistance have been exhausted.'

Despite his deteriorating situation, he then followed his usual custom of holding a daily staff conference, on his way to the conference room making a brief inspection above ground. Clouds of smoke and dust blocked his view of the sea; but he was unaware of the

Pantelleria. The thorough air and naval bombardment devastated the island,
Below: the troop landings went virtually unopposed

Vickers Wellington II
Engines: Two Rolls-Royce Merlin X, 1,075 hp *Armament:* Four .303-inch
Browning machine guns and up to 4,000 lbs of bombs *Maximum speed:* 270 mph
at 17,750 feet *Ceiling:* 23,500 feet *Range:* 2,200 miles max *Weight empty:*
22,258 lbs *Weight loaded:* 33,000 lbs *Span:* 86 feet 2 inches *Length:* 64 feet
7 inches

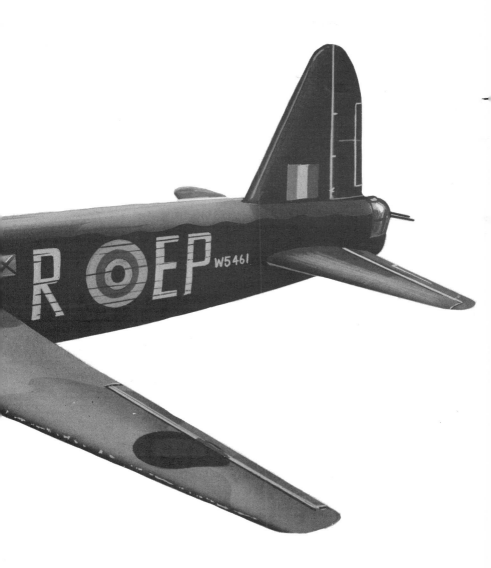

A Sherman grinding through the docks at Pantelleria

Allied armada offshore.

During the discussion at the staff conference, everyone was in agreement. The island was no longer tenable because of a lack of water, the danger of disease, and a shortage of ammunition. No Axis planes remained on Pantelleria – they had been shot down or flown off to safety – no help could be expected from the outside, and everyone, civilians and military alike, was at the end of his endurance.

Pavasi then ordered his air commander to display a large white cross on the airfields to signify capitulation. Because it would take about two hours for news of his surrender decision to reach all posts, Pavasi set the time for the cessation of hostilities at 11 am after which he went above ground. The clouds suddenly opened. He saw the Allied ships offshore.

This was about the time the landing craft were starting their final run to the beaches, and there was a strange almost reassuring silence – except for the noise of the assault craft engines and the drone of a flight of fighters overhead; but not for long. At eleven o'clock, Allied cruisers opened fire at shore battery positions and 30 minutes later destroyers added their shells.

There was no reply from the island and no way to make known the desire of the garrison to surrender. The large white cross had still not appeared on the airfield at 11.35 am and American Flying Fortresses bombed the island in what an observer called 'the most perfect precision bombing of unimaginable intensity'.

Ten minutes later, the commander of the control vessels released the landing craft; at noontime British troops were ashore without opposition. White flags were flying on some of the gutted, ruined buildings, and before long, white sheets would be showing on most.

At Lampedusa, the commander paid no attention to the Allied surrender ultimatum, except to notify Rome: 'Bombardments are continuing without interruption, both from the air and from the sea,' he said. 'Air support required urgently' – but the only help

that came was a stirring exhortation. We are convinced,' Rome radioed, that you will inflict the greatest possible damage on the enemy. Long live Italy.'

Resentful because he believed he had been abandoned; feeling, like Pavasi, that he had done his duty to the best of his ability, the island commander ordered white flags raised in surrender.

Linoso fell the next day. Lampione was unoccupied.

Despite the claims of Fascist propaganda, the islands had been defended by old and inexperienced soldiers, many of whom had their homes there and who, when the Allies attacked, preferred to look after their families; in any case, against the power of the Allied ships and planes, they could have done little with the inadequate and obsolete equipment available to them.

On 20th June British aircraft began to operate from Lampedusa, and six days later, a group of American P-40 fighters was based at Pantelleria.

Eisenhower's laboratory experiment was a success. He had obtained a safer channel for shipping in the central Mediterranean and valuable airfields closer to Sicily.

The day after Pantelleria fell, Mussolini made a speech in Rome. Alluding to the loss of Pantelleria, he explained it by saying that air bombardment, like artillery, conquered ground and allowed infantry to occupy it. What he left unsaid, for there was no need to be explicit, was that the Allies had an overwhelming superiority in artillery, planes, and other weapons and equipment, and if Pantelleria signified that the battle for the Italian homeland had begun, it was a depressing start. Whether the Allies turned next to Sicily, Sardinia, or the mainland, there was little prospect of repelling an invasion.

To the Italian people who had long been weary of the war, wanting an end of the bombings, the hardships, the sorrow and pain, and who had clung to the promise of victory, Pantelleria came as a shock. Even the military forces lost confidence and the hope of eventual triumph. Mussolini's prestige declined among his German allies, his own military establishment, his political colleagues, and, most of all, his

people, who were thoroughly fed up. The Fascist system, it was becoming ever clearer, was nothing more than a big bluff, a hollow shell, a shadow without substance.

As defeatism spread, King Victor Emmanuel III told Mussolini to terminate the alliance with the Germans and make peace with the Allies; but he wished to do so honourably, only with German consent, for he was concerned not only with the proper protocol but also with avoiding German retaliation to what he was sure the Germans would consider a treacherous defection. No one in Italy, he believed, was so clever or so powerful as Mussolini; no one else could solve so well the enormously difficult and delicate problem of ending the alliance and withdrawing from the war.

The alliance, a pact between the National Socialist and Fascist régimes, was in reality a personal union of the two dictators, Hitler and Mussolini, each the head of government and supreme commander of his armed forces. But the close co-operation and mutual assistance they pledged in what Mussolini had called their parallel wars had become a one-way street – the Germans were giving, the Italians receiving weapons, equipment, fuel, and troop units.

The build-up of German forces in Italy coincided with the increasing power and influence of Field-Marshal Albert Kesselring. Sent to Italy at the head of the German Second Air Corps in December 1941, appointed to command all the German armed forces in Italy in October 1942 when the Germans sensed the beginning of increased Allied activity in the Mediterranean area, his control extended in January, 1943, to include the two German armies in Tunisia, Kesselring was 'theatre commander', Hitler's military representative to Mussolini, and point of contact with the Italian Armed Forces High Command, Comando Supremo.

Because Hitler admired Mussolini, he submitted to the pretence of respecting Italian hegemony in the Mediterranean area. German troops were consequently placed under the nominal command of the Italians, but the presence of Kesselring insured the protection of German interests; and the Italians accepted the view that it was better to obtain German co-operation than to impose strict Italian authority.

As German influence in Italy grew, Mussolini had increasing doubts that military victory was possible. He suggested to Hitler that the Axis powers make a separate peace with the Soviet Union or at least withdraw their forces to a shorter, defensible line in the USSR, in order to concentrate their strength against the Anglo-Americans. But Hitler would brook no interference with his holy war against Bolshevism.

Disenchanted, Mussolini in February 1943 appointed Generale d'Armata Vittorio Ambrosio head of Comando Supremo. Ambrosio's dual task, Mussolini specified, was to bring home from far-flung commitments in Russia and the Balkans as many Italian divisions as possible; and to stand up to the Germans. The close and cordial personal and official relationships that had marked the co-operation of German and Italian military men ended.

In February and March, tensions between the Axis partners were aggravated as Mussolini pressed Hitler to make an end to the war in the east, as Ambrosio and the German Armed Forces High Command (the Oberkommando der Wehrmacht, called OKW) wrangled over the sharing of military duties in the Balkans; and as the Italian war machine began to break down for lack of German supplies.

Part of the trouble was that the Axis by then was on the defensive and had no clear strategy on how to gain victory. Submarine warfare was the only offensive German activity that remained effective, and even the Luftwaffe ceased to be a significant force in the war. By May, the combined German and Italian air forces in the Mediterranean area had less than 1,000 planes, and many were obsolescent or entirely obsolete. Hundreds had been destroyed on the ground because of failure to disperse and to camouflage effectively and also because of ineffective anti-aircraft weapons. Even the powerful Italian battle fleet lay immobilized at La

Field-Marshal Albert Kesselring, German military commander in Italy

35

Spezia for lack of fuel.

Ambrosio saw hope for Italy only if Mussolini could break the alliance with Germany. But the Fascist régime was secure only as long as the prospect of victory beckoned and without the Germans, victory was impossible. If Mussolini was going to break with the Germans, the fewer German troops there were in Italy, the better; if he was going to oppose Allied invasion, more German troops were indispensable.

Ambrosio, Mussolini, and the Fascist state were in a quandary.

As Mussolini's personal popularity diminished, so did Italian morale. Clandestine political parties became more vigorous and the first overt labour strike since the establishment of the Fascist state took place in March, while labour unions openly held May Day demonstrations.

The Germans had no illusions about Italian strength. A report on the combat efficiency of the Italian armed forces in May was brutally frank. The Italians, OKW said, 'have not up to now fulfilled the missions assigned them in this war' and have actually failed everywhere' because of inadequate and insufficient weapons and equipment, faulty officer training, and lack of spirit among the troops stemming from a belief in their eventual defeat.

Yet the Germans would not abandon the Italians, for it would cost less to support and strengthen them than to fill the vacuum they would create if they withdrew altogether from the war.

In June, therefore, Hitler said he was willing to send more planes, tanks, self-propelled guns, and troop units to help the Italians defend their country. Although additional German troops stationed in Italy would make it resemble an occupied territory, the fall of Pantelleria persuaded Ambrosio, with Mussolini's concurrence, to accept more assistance. By the end of June, there were five German divisions in Italy. Two were in Sicily.

The Italian Sixth Army headquarters, with training and coastal defense duties, had been in Sicily since the autumn of 1941, but in the spring of 1943, when the Tunisian campaign ended, its responsibilities were extended. The army commander was named also the Armed Forces Commander, Sicily, with control over the tactical commitment of Army, Navy, Air, and Reserve elements and of the German ground troops there. Through a high commissioner for civilian affairs, the commander also controlled the administration of nine provincial prefects. German air and naval elements remained separate and under German control.

In May 1943, a new commander was appointed. He was Generale d'Armata Alfredo Guzzoni, who had been in retirement for two years and was 66 years old. He had never been to Sicily, nor had he ever displayed the slightest interest in the island. But he was a dedicated and highly professional soldier. His chief of staff, Colonel Emilio Faldello, was young and capable but also a stranger to Sicily. Contrary to Italian doctrine governing the selection of commander and chief of staff, Guzzoni and Faldello had never before served together, but in Sicily they would make a good team.

When Guzzoni inspected the state of affairs in Sicily, he was shocked. He had few anti-naval guns, only one anti-tank gun for every five miles of coast, and deficiencies in all types of artillery. He needed 8,000 tons of supplies daily for his civilian and military requirements, but was receiving between 1,500 and 2,000. Civilian morale was low because of Allied air bombings, restricted food supplies, and widespread black marketeering. So far as Guzzoni could see, everyone wanted only to end the war.

The Italian forces under him numbered about 200,000 men organized into four infantry divisions and a variety of coastal units totalling perhaps the equivalent of eight divisions. The coastal battalions, which had the mission of repelling invaders at the water's edge, were composed of older men, were usually badly commanded, often had responsibilities for sectors far too large for their capabilities, in some cases a shoreline 25 miles in length; they had virtually no transportation and for the most part antiquated guns and equipment. Even the superior infantry divisions were none too good. The Aosta and Napoli Divisions were poorly trained and,

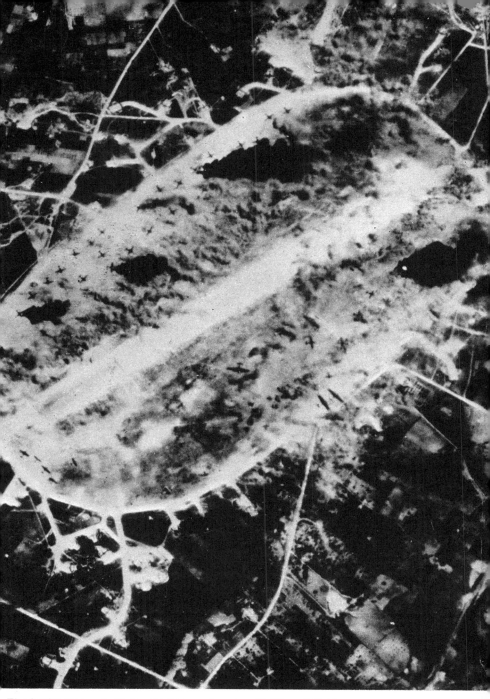

The 'softening up'. Flying Fortresses bomb a Sicilian airfield

The German presence. *Above:* Laying telephone wires. *Below:* German flak guns guard obsolescent Italian fighters

together with the Assietta Division, operated with reduced organizational strength and equipment. Only the Livorno Division was at authorized strength and had a full complement of organic transportation. But in all four divisions, artillery ammunition was non-existent or in very short supply, and communications varied from poor to altogether inadequate.

The three naval bases in Sicily were equipped with anti-naval and anti-aircraft artillery, and their seaward defences were effectively organized. But undependable reservists manned many guns, and most of the pieces were old, of small calibre, and short in range. There was little preparation for defence against an attack from the landward side.

Except at the naval bases, no continuous system of coastal defences existed. Obstacles, minefields, anti-tank ditches, and concrete fortifications were widely separated. Many defence posts lacked garrisons, weapons, and troop shelters, which were, when they existed, poorly camouflaged. In the interior, only a few roadblocks had been erected, most of them inefficiently. An inland blocking line behind the coastal fortifications, supposed to be a strong barrier, consisted of a carefully traced, coloured-pencil mark on a map.

The 30,000 German troops on the island were something else. The 15th Panzer Grenadier Division commanded by Major-General Eberhard Rodt and the Hermann Göring Division under Major-General Paul Conrath were well trained and equipped. They operated under Guzzoni's command, but Panzer General Hans Valentine Hube's XIV Panzer Corps headquarters, located in southern Italy, administered and supplied them. Lieutenant-General Fridolin von Senger und Etterlin was the liaison officer with Sixth Army to co-ordinate the employment of German troops.

A single unified headquarters known as Commandant Messina Strait under Colonel Ernest Günther Baade brought together German Army, Navy, and Air Force installations in that area and was responsible for transportation, a ferry service from the mainland, depots, and about 70 anti-aircraft batteries sited on both sides of the strait.

Guzzoni could expect no assistance from the Axis naval forces. It was doubtful that Mussolini would dare commit the battle fleet, and even if he did, it would take the warships a day to reach Sicilian waters from La Spezia. The Germans had only a flotilla of small boats at Messina.

Nor could Guzzoni anticipate much help from the air. The Italian air force was hopeless because of obsolete and inferior aircraft and indeed after the fall of Tunisia in May, the Italian bombers withdrew from Sicily to the mainland. The Germans took over the protection of Sicily from their own airfields, but they sustained heavy losses in May and June because of the numerical and technical inferiority of their planes.

The weakness of the Axis air and naval forces put the entire burden of defending Sicily on the ground forces. Because the Italian units lacked mobility when compared to the German formations, Guzzoni decided to have the Italian forces meet and hold invaders near the beaches until the locations of the main Allied attacks were recognized; then the German divisions would counterattack and drive the invaders into the sea.

Guzzoni therefore established his headquarters near Enna in the centre of the island. The XVI Corps under Generale di Corpo d'Armata Caeto Rossi defended the eastern half of the island with the Napoli and Livorno Divisions. The XII Corps under Generale di Corpo d'Armata Francesco Zingales looked after the western half with the Aosta and Assietta Divisions. The 15th Panzer Grenadier Division was split into three task forces with the bulk of its strength in the west. The Hermann Göring Division, divided into two combat teams, was orientated to the south and east.

Expecting the Allies to attack in the middle of July, Guzzoni would do the best he could; but he was dubious about the outcome of the battle, for he felt much like a colleague who said: 'We may be able to put up an honourable defence against a large-scale landing, but we have no chance to repel the enemy.'

Unless, of course, the Germans sent massive help.

The landings

Above and far right: The British landings in the Gulf of Noto. There was no resistance

The Germans might have put more than two divisions into Sicily had they not been deceived and misled by the Allied cover operations, which were designed to disguise the intention of invading Sicily and to prompt German expectation of landings in Sardinia and Greece instead. A significant part of the deception was 'the man who never was', contrived by British intelligence. A soldier who had died of pneumonia and whose lungs and general condition would indicate death by drowning was dressed as an officer-courier, and with an official briefcase chained to a wrist, the body was set adrift by a submarine off the coast of neutral Spain where the currents would wash it ashore, ostensibly the victim of an aircraft crash at sea. Three days later, London received

word that the body had been delivered to the British Naval Attaché in Madrid, but not before a fictitious letter in the briefcase had been opened and read, presumably by friends of the Germans. The letter instructed Alexander to feint at Sicily while preparing to invade Sardinia; it directed General Sir H. Maitland Wilson, the commander in the Middle East, to veil his thrust against Greece by simulating action against the Dodecanese Islands. Accepting these orders as authentic, the Germans strengthened their coastal defences in Sardinia and Greece.

The Allies in North Africa, meanwhile, prepared their invasion of Sicily. A concentrated assault on the southeastern portion of the island did not mean that the troops would come

ashore bunched together. Rather it signified that more than seven divisions, preceded by parts of two airborne divisions dropping inland, would land simultaneously along a shore of 100 miles, Montgomery's forces on 30 miles of beach, Patton's on a 70 mile front. In terms of frontage and initial assault forces, the invasion of Sicily was much larger and far more dispersed than the landings in Normandy a year later.

Montgomery's Eighth Army would open its invasion with glider troops landing to take Ponte Grande to facilitate the seizure of Syracuse; they were also, if possible, to capture nearby coastal batteries and a seaplane base. For four days later, Commando troops were to come in by sea to eliminate a major coastal battery at Cape Murro di Porci, several miles south of Syracuse, and only then would come the main assault.

Lieutenant-General Sir Miles C. Dempsey's XIII Corps would have the 5th Division going ashore to seize Cassibile, then turning north to take Syracuse; the 59th Division would take Avola and protect the corps left flank. Lieutenant-General Sir Oliver Leese's XXX Corps was to send the 231st Infantry Brigade Group, the 51st Division, and the 1st Canadian Division against the Pachino peninsula. After making contact with the Americans near Ragusa, Leese was to push to Palazzolo, then to Vizzini; he was also to extend his responsibility northward along the east coast to permit Dempsey to move the bulk of his strength to the north against Augusta, then Catania.

The invasion by Patton's Seventh Army would begin with the parachute drop of a reinforced regiment of the 82nd Airborne Division on Piano Lupo, about in the middle of the army's

The DUKW. An amphibian vehicle of almost legendary versatility, the DUKW took part in the Sicily landings, and almost every other landing on the mainland of Europe, in its role as a stores or personnel carrier. *Length:* 31 feet. *Beam:* 8 feet. *Engine:* 104 horse power GMC. *Speed:* 50 mph (land); 5.4 knots (water) *Range:* 240 miles (land); 50 miles (water). *Crew:* 2. *Payload:* 5,000 pounds. *Armament:* One .30 machine gun

beach frontage and several miles inland from Gela; the paratroopers were to block enemy approaches to the beaches during the early hours of the landings when the amphibious troops were especially vulnerable. Then would come three simultaneous seaborne assaults. The two on the right were under the control of Major-General Omar N. Bradley's II Corps – the 45th Division was to come ashore near the fishing village of Scoglitti, the 1st Division at Gela. On the left, operating independently, was the reinforced 3rd Division, which would land at Licata.

The British hoped to get three major ports quickly – Syracuse, Augusta, and Catania; but the Americans would have none – only the minor ports of Licata and Gela. But what made beach unloading seem feasible was a new vehicle called the DUKW, a 2½-ton amphibious truck, which could bring supplies and equipment from Liberty ships anchored a few miles offshore directly to dumps and depots on the beach.

Even more important for the amphibious assault would be the large-scale use for the first time in an actual operation of a new series of landing ships and craft. Flat-bottomed vessels with hinged bow that fell forward to form a ramp, they would come aground and discharge men, tanks, and vehicles quickly and directly to the beach. Developed as the result of combined British and American initiative and effort, they would permit the near-perfection of one of the most complicated military techniques, an amphibious assault against a hostile shore.

Once the troops reached Sicily and secured their initial objectives, what then? Alexander made no firm plans beyond the landings, but in a general way he expected Montgomery to make the main effort and drive quickly through Catania to Messina. Patton was to have the clearly subsidiary and subordinate task of protecting Montgomery's flank and rear.

This division of responsibilities in the campaign reflected Alexander's estimate of the relative combat

The initial Allied assault on Sicily: Operation 'Husky'

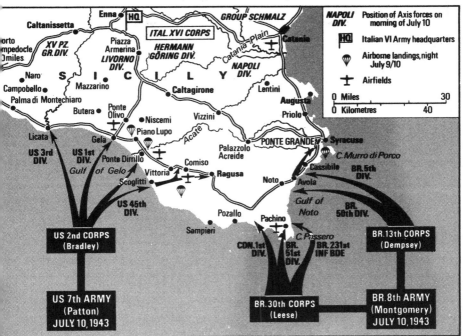

effectiveness of British and American units. Having become acquainted with the American ground forces in Tunisia during the disastrous battle of Kasserine Pass, where he had been depressed by American inexperience and general ineptitude, he preferred to have the veteran troops of Montgomery's army in the most important endeavour – getting to Messina.

Cunningham reported that some Americans were, as he said, 'very sore' to be relegated to a secondary role in the campaign, and it was true – commanders felt somewhat humiliated. Although several of Patton's colleagues urged him to protest, he refused, saying that an order was an order and he would do his 'goddamndest to carry it out' whether he liked it or not.

When the Tunisian campaign ended in mid-May, Eisenhower selected the time and the date for the invasion of Sicily. His choice was largely dictated by the phase of the moon, for the airborne troops needed some light for their operations, while the naval forces required total darkness for the

approach of their convoys to the target areas. The night of 9th July satisfied both. The airborne elements, then, would land in Sicily shortly after midnight, 9th July. The seaborne elements would hit the beaches at 2.45 am, 10th July.

As soon as the Tunisian campaign was over, the Allied air forces began to attack Sicily, bombing military targets throughout the island, and concentrating on the groups of airfields clustered in the west. Then, during the final week before the invasion, they shifted to the eastern fields; enemy air opposition, the pilots found, was surprisingly light.

For the invasion itself, the air forces mustered 670 first-line aircraft based on the islands of Pantelleria, Gozo, and Malta, and on 12 airfields in the Cape Bon peninsula of Tunisia. They would furnish a constant umbrella of flights over the landing beaches, meanwhile keeping the bulk of their strength in hand and ready to be massed against the enemy wherever planes might be needed.

45

By dawn on 10th July, all British assault troops were ashore. Here supplies are unloaded, and the beach prepared for vehicle traffic

Transporting the assault troops to Sicily were about 3,500 vessels of all types organized into two task forces, one under Vice-Admiral Henry K. Hewitt, the other under Vice-Admiral Sir Bertram H. Ramsay. The vessels sailed from several ports in North Africa at different times according to a meticulous schedule that took into account the varying speeds of the ships and craft, the requirements of security, and the desire to have the troops travel in as much comfort as possible.

The ships reached their rendezvous points on the morning of 9th July just as the wind began to rise and churn the sea; from a velocity of 10 miles per hour, a westward wind increased by afternoon to a maximum blow of about 40 miles per hour. As the ships rolled and bucked, many soldiers, especially those crowded into LCIs, became seasick, hardly a fit condition to fight.

Late that afternoon, when the ships turned north for their final approach,

they took the wind and seas broadside. Columns and formations loosened, cargoes shifted, courses and speeds had to be altered. All the convoys were thus about an hour late arriving at the assigned areas offshore after darkness, and many vessels were stationed improperly.

Eisenhower and Alexander had gone to Malta to await the reports of the operation in Cunningham's underground headquarters. They discussed whether they ought to postpone the landings for another 24 hours because of the weather, but in the end they decided to go ahead. Perhaps the gale would lull the enemy into believing that an invasion was impossible. Perhaps, as a result, the invasion would come as a complete surprise: any advantage would be welcome.

Although a few Allied planners ventured the guess that the Italian defenders would be a pushover because their arms and equipment were well below German standards, most expected them to resist strenuously. Not

only were the Italians bolstered by German troops; they would also be fighting in defence of their homeland. Getting ashore might be very tough.

Mostly because the weather was excellent and entirely conducive to amphibious operations during the first ten days of July, the Germans and Italians in Sicily and Rome began to sense, almost by intuition but ever more strongly, that the Allies were up to something. When intelligence reports indicated that the vast preponderance of Allied landing craft and airplanes were in positions threatening Sardinia, Sicily, and the southern mainland of Italy, their feelings seemed confirmed. By 5th July commanders and staffs were on edge. Fires started by Allied bombardments were being mistaken for landings in progress, and a host of messages relating to imaginary invasions kept headquarters busy and in a perpetual state of alarm. The wait became unbearable.

On 8th July when Guzzoni ordered the ports of Licata, Porto Empedocle, and Sciacca on the southern shore prepared for demolition, authorities in Rome ordered earth and rock to be dumped into the harbours of Trapani and Marsala and their docks destroyed.

The nervousness that came from the unknown was dissipated somewhat on the morning of 9th July when Luftwaffe reconnaissance patrols reported the presence in the Mediterranean of convoys formed of landing craft and transports. They were travelling at high speed in waters not far from Pantelleria and although their direction gave no certainty of the destination, Guzzoni concluded that the invasion of Sicily was at hand. He became even more sure that afternoon when he received a message reporting the movement of additional convoys.

At 7 pm, although Guzzoni could not know that the aircraft towing the British glider troops were forming up over the North African coast, he ordered the troops in Sicily into a preliminary alert.

Shortly thereafter Allied airplanes bombed Caltanissetta, Syracuse, Palazzolo Acreide, and Catania, causing severe damage. When the aircraft withdrew, Allied warships struck Syracuse, Catania, Taormina, Tra-

The American landing: confidence and technology combined in the biggest amphibious operation of the war

Above: **Paratroopers advancing.**
Opposite: **Colonel 'Jim' Gavin,
the paratroop commander (*right*)**

pani, and Augusta with long-range naval gunfire. There could no longer be any doubt that an invasion was impending. At 10 pm, although he had no way of knowing that the American paratroopers had departed North Africa an hour earlier, Guzzoni placed his units on full alert.

During the night, the waters off the Sicilian shores seemed deserted. The wind continued high, the sea rough – yet there was every indication of a forthcoming invasion. Where would the Allies try to land? And would the Italo-German forces be able to drive them back?

If these questions raised anxieties, at least one related issue had been favourably resolved and the good news reached Guzzoni, as well as Comando Supremo in Rome, that afternoon. Hitler had, upon being informed of the imminent landings, directed that the 1st Parachute Division, stationed in France, be made ready for immediate transfer by air to Sicily. If ordered,

the entire division could be moved in five days, but the fact that Hitler had reacted without hesitation to strengthen the defences of Sicily meant that other German forces, perhaps the 29th Panzer Grenadier Division in southern Italy, might become available even sooner.

Shortly after midnight, in the first hour of 10th July, one kind of tension broke, another sort set in. Guzzoni received word of airborne landings. The report was vague and no precise numbers or area was given – but convinced that the invasion had at last begun, Guzzoni issued a proclamation exhorting the soldiers and civilians in Sicily to repel the landings. At the same time, he ordered the Gela pier destroyed. By 1.45 am, reports of so many airborne landings in so many different areas had reached Guzzoni that he specifically warned his corps commanders to expect landings all along the southern and eastern shorelines of the island.

What was happening was that most of the American paratroopers, as well as those British glidermen who had landed unharmed, were spread over a

tremendous region. Coalescing into small groups, they roamed through the rear areas of the Italian coastal units, cutting communications, ambushing small reconnaissance parties, and creating an inordinate amount of confusion. Most of these soldiers had very little idea of where they were – for a while, Brigadier-General James Gavin, the American regimental com-

mander, was not even sure he was in Sicily. But they overran pillboxes guarding crossroads, seized bridges, and generally gave the impression that they were in far larger numbers than they actually were.

The wind and waves in the Gulf of Noto were far less disturbing than elsewhere around Sicily, and most of the initial assault units of the British

The LCM. This landing craft could be used to land vehicles, stores, or men, but due to its comparatively low pay load, it was usually used to transport personnel. *Weight:* 21 tons. *Length:* 44 feet. *Beam:* 14 feet. *Engines:* Two 60 horse power diesels. *Payload:* 16 tons. *Crew:* 7. *Speed:* 7½ knots. *Range:* 56 miles

army came ashore close to the scheduled time. Small landing craft brought troops to the beaches, and they were followed by larger craft and by landing ships carrying supporting artillery and tanks. Warships stood offshore ready to pound Italian coastal defences into submission. Overhead, fighter planes were on their way to cover the landings and ward off expected aerial blows against Allied shipping and assault beaches; and starting at daylight and every half hour thereafter, formations of fighter-bombers would attack the main roads leading to the assault beaches in order to discourage and disrupt counter-attacks.

Montgomery's seaborne landings were uniformly successful. The first

The LVT (or LCT, Landing Craft, Tanks). This heavy landing craft was designed specifically to transport and land tanks, although it could of course be used to land other vehicles, stores and men, as well. *Weight:* 350 tons. *Length:* 192 feet. *Beam:* 31 feet. *Engines:* Two 500 horse power Paxman diesels. *Speed:* 10½ knots. *Range:* 1,900 miles. *Crew:* 2 officers and 10 men. *Payload:* Five 40-ton tanks. *Armament:* Two 40mm Bofors

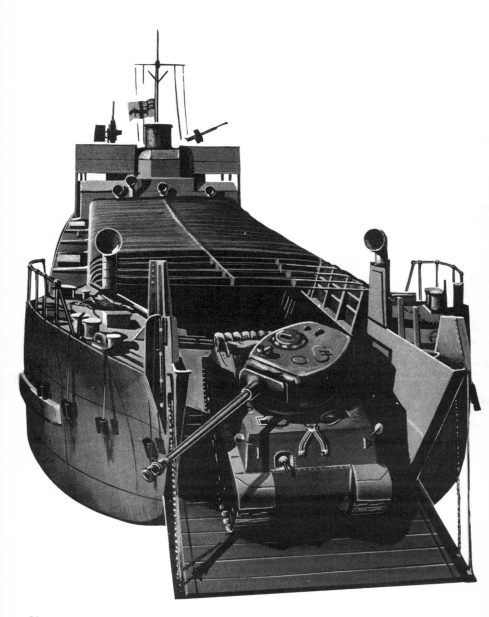

waves gained tactical surprise and swept over most of the coastal defence units almost before the defenders were aware of the assault and there was thus hardly any co-ordinated opposition. When coastal batteries and inland artillery pieces opened fire and struck the invasion sites, naval guns, together with the rapid movement of troops inland, quickly silenced them.

At 4 am Guzzoni received a phone call from the commander of Naval Base Messina. He said that a message sent by the German radio station in Syracuse indicated that Allied glider troops had inundated the east coast and were attacking the Syracuse seaplane base. Guzzoni immediately instructed the XVI Corps commander, Rossi, to rush ground troops to the Augusta-Syracuse area.

The news, plus previous information from reconnaissance aircraft that Allied ships were off the southern coast as well, led Guzzoni to conclude that the Allies would land or were already landing simultaneously in many places. Unable to counter all the landings, he committed his available reserves to the sites he considered most dangerous to the overall defence of the island – Syracuse, Gela, and Licata. Syracuse was by far the most important, for it gave access to Catania and ultimately to Messina, but Guzzoni figured that the reinforced German regiment (called Group Schmalz), and the Napoli Division nearby, together with the strong defences of the naval base, would probably prevent an Allied breakthrough into the Catania plain. He therefore ordered the bulk of the Hermann Göring Division to mass against invaders coming ashore near Gela.

The Seventh Army landings in the Gulf of Gela were much more difficult because of the westerly gale. The wind delayed the naval task forces pushing their way through heavy seas to their landing craft release points and all the ships were somewhat disorganized when they arrived. One convoy was seriously behind schedule, and, as a consequence, the 45th Division landings near Scoglitti were postponed one hour; but the other landings by the 3rd and 1st Divisions, at Licata and Gela respectively, went ahead close to the timetable even though it was most difficult to hoist out and launch the landing craft that took the assault waves to shore.

There was almost constant fire from shore at first, but naval bombardment was the immediate answer to this interference. On the Licata mole, a railroad battery mounting four cannon on an armoured train was a serious obstacle until a series of naval volleys destroyed the train and the guns. When a searchlight fixed its beam on landing boats moving toward Gela, a destroyer knocked the light out in five salvos, smashed a second light in three. At Scoglitti, a fairly heavy swell made the ships pitch and roll and dispersed and disorganized the assault waves; but the troops coming ashore found only scattered resistance by units that had suffered prior ravage from roaming bands of paratroopers.

The Italian coastal gunners remained at their pieces far longer than might have been expected, given the relative impotence of their weapons as compared to the Allied firepower. The Gela pier had been demolished in accordance with Guzzoni's order – the great flash and loud explosion occurring as two Ranger battalions were sailing toward it – but all in all, the Americans arrived in Sicily with much less difficulty than had been anticipated. Although Italian shells continued to fall on some invasion beaches long after daylight, although the first Axis planes appeared over the shipping massed in front of the assault beaches at 4.30 am and sank two vessels, increasing number of American troops and growing piles of supplies ashore attested to the success of the initial landings.

No one yet knew that the important high ground ahead of Gela, Piano Lupo and its important road junction, was not in the firm possession of American paratroopers. And that was where Guzzoni ordered troops to concentrate for an attack against the American beach-head.

The Axis reaction

Around daylight of 10th July as the scope and strength of the Allied landings became evident, Guzzoni was convinced that there was little likelihood that the Allies would undertake additional amphibious operations in the western part of the island. Even if they did, the forces defending Sicily had enough to do to counter those in the southeastern region – first, to contain them pending the possible arrival of reinforcements from the mainland; second, to drive them into the sea; and third, at the very least to hold open the escape route through Messina. Thus, Guzzoni ordered the 15th Panzer Grenadier Division, which had moved to the west only a few days before the invasion, to retrace its steps and return to the centre of the island, where it would be in good position for commitment in any sector. He also instructed the Hermann Göring Division (except for Group Schmalz, which had plenty to do in the Syracuse area), the XVI Corps headquarters, and the Livorno Division to counter attack the Americans before they could stake out, consolidate, and fortify a beach-head.

Unfortunately for Guzzoni, he could not be sure that his instructions were received by all the units involved. Telephone communications had been poor to begin with, and many wires had been cut by American paratroopers and Allied bombs. As a consequence, some units failed to receive specific orders, and they proceeded to act on their own initiative in accordance with the defensive doctrine that had been generally established for the island. Instead of a concerted and massive push against the Americans, there would be small and unco-ordinated, largely independent, thrusts. But even these would prove dangerous.

Conrath, the Hermann Göring Division commander, had learned of the American landings early that morning, not from Guzzoni but from Kesselring's headquarters near Rome. The news was confirmed when several of his reconnaissance patrols encountered and clashed with American paratroopers near Niscemi. Still later, when he received word that Schmalz was moving against the British landings, Conrath decided that the time had come to carry out the defensive

plan. He would launch a counter-attack at Gela.

Because his telephone communications with Sixth Army and the XVI Corps had been cut early that morning Conrath used the independent German network to call von Senger, the liaison officer at Guzzoni's headquarters. He outlined his plan and said he would jump off without delay; von Senger approved and said he would notify Guzzoni.

At 4 am Conrath got his movement under way, as two reinforced regiments, one heavy in infantry, the other heavy in tanks, set out on three country roads from the Caltagirone area to assembly points south of Biscari and Niscemi, where they would form up and strike at Gela from the east. The march turned out to be difficult – the roads were extremely poor, air strikes interfered, and the ubiquitous American paratroopers put up obstacles. Confusion and recurring delays ensued. Five hours after beginning to move, the columns were still struggling toward their assembly areas.

Rossi, the XVI Corps commander,

did much better. He sent an Italian regiment named Mobile Group E by truck from Niscemi in two columns towards Piano Lupo, from which centre the Group was to hit Gela generally from the northeast. Half way to Piano Lupo, at Casa del Priolo, Mobile Group E ran into about 100 American paratroopers who had reduced a strongpoint early that morning and had set up a blocking position.

The Americans allowed the point of one column, three small vehicles, to enter their lines before opening fire and killing or capturing the occupants. The sound of firing halted the main body of Mobile Group E.

Thirty minutes later, two Italian infantry companies moved out in extended attack formation toward the Americans, who waited until the Italians were 200 yards away before opening a withering fire of rifles, thickened by the bullets of numerous machine guns they had captured at the strongpoint. The fusillade pinned down the Italians, except for a few in the rear who managed to get back to the main column.

The firing having revealed that the

Left: Panzer Grenadiers on the move. *Above:* A Panzer Grenadier carrying an MG-34, adapted for anti-aircraft fire

Americans lacked cannon, the Italians moved an artillery piece to a hill just out of range of the paratroopers' weapons. As this gun opened fire, an American patrol previously dispatched to Piano Lupo returned and reported that no strong enemy force held the junction. Only a few Italians were there, and they were armed with machine guns in a dug-in position protected by barbed wire.

Unable to counter the fire of the single Italian artillery piece, the Americans decided to pull back to Piano Lupo, where they would be closer to the forces coming ashore amphibiously, and as they moved out of Casa del Priolo, naval shells began to come down on the Italian column. They were being put out in response to calls from troops nearer Gela who had spotted Mobile Group E – but since the paratroopers had no way of controlling or directing the naval fire, they moved to the south in a wide skirting retirement.

The Americans gone, the Italians advanced to Piano Lupo, reaching the place a few minutes ahead of the paratroopers, who remained hidden. Passing through the naval fire that continued intermittently, about 20 Italian tanks went through the road junction and down the hill toward Gela, while the infantrymen of Mobile Group E remained deployed at Piano Lupo. The tanks soon ran into Americans coming up from the Gela beaches, and the two leading tanks were quickly knocked out, their destruction disrupting the movement of the column, which halted. Without infantry support and under a growing volume of fire from warships, the Italians turned back and rejoined the infantry at Piano Lupo; then the entire force pulled back and took positions in the foothills bordering the Gela plain.

With the Italians gone, the paratroopers reduced the small Italian position at Piano Lupo and made contact with troops advancing from the beaches.

Meanwhile, the Livorno Division launched a two-pronged attack against Gela from the northwest. About 20 tanks came down the Butera road, and although seven or eight were knocked out by naval gunfire, the rest dashed into the town, where a deadly game of hide and seek took place. American Rangers darted in and out of buildings, throwing hand grenades and firing rocket launchers at the tanks, which found themselves at a disadvantage not only because of the narrow streets but also because no infantrymen had accompanied them. After about half an hour, the tanks withdrew from the city, every one that managed to escape to Butera carrying a high proportion of wounded men.

Only then did about 600 infantrymen of the Livorno Division move toward Gela in a courageous but nonsensical attack. In almost normal, parade-ground formation, they advanced with precision despite terrifying casualties torn in their ranks by the fire of American rifles, machine guns, and mortars. Not a single soldier reached Gela, and having taken enormous losses the men fell back.

On the other side of Gela, Conrath's troops were finally in position south of Niscemi at 2 pm. They launched their attack against Gela, but their forward movement was quickly stopped by American infantrymen supported by naval shells that came whistling in, and although Conrath personally tried to get the attack started again at three o'clock, it was without success. An hour later he called off his effort and pulled back.

Around six o'clock, the Americans who had halted the Hermann Göring Division reported enthusiastically: 'Tanks are withdrawing, it seems we are too much for them.'

There was scattered fighting in the American zone throughout the evening, but by nightfall, the Americans had Licata, Gela, and Scoglitti firmly in hand and their beach-head was well established, with more troops, artillery, tanks, and supplies flowing ashore in a constant stream. Yet it seemed that the Italian and German actions on the first day were little more than probes designed to locate and fix the invaders. There would inevitably be additional attempts, stronger and more concerted, to push the Americans into the sea.

The British troops were easily ashore on the eastern face of Sicily. They badly hurt the widely dispersed Napoli Division and, against decreasing resistance, pushed to their objectives. Unloading over the beaches went slowly but steadily despite enemy air attacks that were annoying rather than damaging.

In the northern part of the beach-head, the 5th Division took Cassibile on the coastal highway by 8 am, though clearing and consolidating operations consumed the rest of the morning and part of the afternoon. Not until about 3 pm could the division start north toward Ponte Grande, where eight officers and 65 men of the Air-landing Brigade had seized and were holding the bridge.

But by this time, the gallant British airborne troops were in desperate

straits. They had battled Italian soldiers, marines, and sailors sent against them from the Augusta-Syracuse naval base all day long, and all but 15 of them were wounded – and at 3.30 pm, almost completely out of ammunition but still resisting, they were overrun. Eight men escaped capture, walked to the south, and made contact with the 5th Division coming up the coastal road.

A column of British infantry, tanks, and artillery moved against the bridge and the Italian force was unable to withstand the armoured vehicles. As the defenders scattered, the British recaptured Ponte Grande intact, the column continuing to Syracuse and entering the city unopposed. Hardly pausing, the troops rolled north toward Augusta. At dusk, they ran into contingents of Group Schmalz, which had rushed down from Catania and had dug good defensive positions midway to Augusta at Priolo. The British halted.

At the end of the first day of the invasion, the British beach-head from Priolo to Pozzallo was firmly established. All indications promised an easy advance to the north, through Augusta and Catania to Messina.

Or so it seemed.

With only incomplete knowledge of the situation on the evening of 10th July Guzzoni dismissed as exaggeration several reports informing him that British troops had taken Syracuse. But he understood perfectly and was disappointed in the failure of the counterattacks against Gela.

At 8 pm he ordered Rossi's XVI Corps headquarters to keep Group Schmalz and the Napoli Division tightly pressed against the British around Syracuse; and to launch the Hermann Göring and Livorno Divisions in a strong counterattack against Gela, this time in a co-ordinated fashion, to eliminate the American beach-head.

Kesselring, lacking communications with Guzzoni and getting his information from Luftwaffe stations at Catania and Taormina, was unaware of Guzzoni's intention to counterattack on 11th July; but when he learned of the fall of Syracuse, he had no doubt of the authenticity of the message and promptly notified Italian authorities in Rome.

This news, plus the general breakdown of the Italian coastal defences, indicated to Kesselring that the Italians were incapable of putting up effective resistance. Convinced that only German units would prove up to the demands of the battle, he sent a message through Luftwaffe channels to Conrath and ordered him to counterattack with the Hermann Göring Division against Gela in the morning.

Conrath, together with Generale di Divisione Domenico Chirieleison, who commanded the Livorno Division, was at Rossi's corps headquarters receiving Guzzoni's orders. Rossi directed that a concerted attack be made at 6 am the Germans to converge on Gela from the northeast in three columns, the Italians to converge on Gela from the northwest in the same way and when Conrath returned to his command post, he thus received Kesselring's order, which gave him double incentive to carry out the counterattack.

At 3 am, Guzzoni learned from von Senger that Syracuse had definitely fallen. Concerned by the overriding need to prevent the British from getting onto the Catania plain and from there quickly to Messina – for that would bottle up all the Axis forces in Sicily – Guzzoni modified his plans. He told Rossi that as soon as the Hermann Göring Division attack showed signs of success, the Germans were to be diverted eastward against the British while the Livorno Division, after taking Gela, was to move westward against Licata.

This obviously weakened the Gela counterattack, for instead of concentrating six columns against the objective, the two division commanders would be looking over their shoulders toward the necessity to shift from a converging attack into a diverging movement.

Nonetheless, Conrath and Chirieleison went ahead with their preparations though Conrath wasn't ready to jump off until 15 minutes after the agreed time. Unable to make contact

Above: Naval fire from offshore played an important part in the American defence of their beachhead. *Below:* An Italian armored car firing on Allied positions.

Above: Italian infantry attacking.
Above and below right: The first
prisoners

by radio or telephone with Chirieleison at 6.15 am he assumed that the
Italians would launch their attack
simultaneously as arranged and so he
sent three task forces of his division
forward.

At the same time, one of Chirieleison's columns, an Italian task force
built around Mobile Group E, apparently seeing the Germans start, opened
its attack. About that time, fortui-
tously, German and Italian aircraft
struck the Gela beaches and the
vessels lying offshore.

Mobile Group E headed directly for
Gela against heavy fire, but despite a
courageous advance the Italians had
to stop and break off after two hours
for their material was unable to stand
up to the pounding of American
artillery and naval guns.

Conrath's tanks and infantry became involved immediately in a
series of scattered battles at very
close range and the attack bogged
down; but Conrath personally re-

grouped his units and sent them forward again. Overrunning or outflanking some of the advance American
positions, the Hermann Göring Division attack was moving ruthlessly
ahead by 9 am but was then struck in
the flank from the east by a group of
American paratroopers led by Gavin.
Conrath responded by diverting part
of his troops against Gavin, while
maintaining most of his pressure
against the beaches near Gela.

By this time, the Livorno Division
was attacking toward the western
part of the town and the entire US 1st
Division area flamed, as infantrymen,
Rangers, engineers, tankers, and artil-
lerymen, supported by warships poured out defensive fire. Unloading operations came to a halt as soldiers formed
hastily improvised firing lines in the
town and along the dunes.

Patton appeared briefly at a command post in Gela, a two-storey
building, and watched the Italian
attack for several minutes. Then as
he turned to leave, he called out to
the soldiers, 'Kill every one of the
goddam bastards.'

The defenders almost did just that.

The naval 6-inch shells that struck the Italian columns were particularly effective, through thick clouds of dust and smoke, Americans could see Italian troops staggering as if dazed. As casualties mounted, the Livorno Division attack stalled. Rangers and infantrymen then moved out to finish off the battle, taking 400 Italians prisoner as the Livorno units pulled back.

The battering received by the Livorno Division temporarily destroyed its effectiveness as a combat unit.

Meanwhile, as the major part of Conrath's tanks moved toward the beaches, the Gela plain became a raging inferno of exploding shells, smoke, and fire. The leading German tanks reached within 2,000 yards of the shoreline and raked supply dumps and landing craft, and with victory apparently within grasp, the division headquarters reported to Guzzoni: 'Pressure by the Hermann Göring Division has forced the enemy to re-embark temporarily.'

Guzzoni was elated. After a brief consultation with von Senger, he instructed Rossi to put the revised

The British take Syracuse on the first day, as planned

plan into action – wheel the German division that afternoon to the east toward Vittoria and have the men continue through the night to Palazzolo Acreide and Syracuse.

But the Herman Göring Division never reached the beaches east of Gela; nor was there thought of American re-embarkation. Artillery duelled with tanks, engineer parties established a firing line, and infantry battled at point-blank range with bazooka and grenade. Naval guns for once remained silent – the opposing forces were too close together for the warships to fire without imperilling American lives.

Pounded by the heavy volume of fire, discouraged because there was no sign of panic among the Americans, the leading German tanks were unable to cross the coastal highway. Behind them, others milled in confusion finally pulling back, slowly at first, then faster, as naval guns opened fire and chased them. Sixteen German tanks were left burning on the Gela plain, and more were destroyed elsewhere, and with one-third of his tanks knocked out or disabled, Conrath called off his attack a little after 2 pm, although fighting continued until late in the evening.

Guzzoni then changed his plans once more. The fierce and stubborn American resistance, the arrival of additional Allied units in Sicily, and pressure in the Vittoria – Comiso area indicated that it would be difficult to get the Hermann Göring Division to the east coast by way of Palazzolo Acreide. That afternoon he ordered the XVI Corps to suspend all offensive action in the Gela area and to withdraw the German division to Caltagirone, as the first step in moving Conrath's troops on the following day, 12th July, to Vizzini for commitment against the British. Rossi was to consolidate the Livorno Division in the Caltagirone area in order to cover the German movement.

Before Guzzoni's instructions reached Conrath, von Senger visited the division. Disappointed because the tanks had not broken through to the beaches, von Senger thought that Conrath could nevertheless go eastward through Vittoria for the Americans, he felt, were so battered after two days of counterattack that they would be unable to contest the movement.

But when Conrath tried to turn and strike to Vittoria, his tanks were so manhandled by a conglomerate force of paratroopers and infantrymen under Gavin that the attack never

Patton in the streets of Gela, 11th July

started. Ignoring von Senger's instructions and following Guzzoni's
orders instead, Conrath withdrew to
the foot-hills south of Niscemi as the
first step in a retirement to Caltagirone – a move he would make in
several stages.

The Americans that evening, despite
the heavy losses sustained by the 1st
Division in the Gela area, had cause to
be satisfied. Of the 60 tanks that
had smashed against them around
Gela, they had knocked out more than
), the 45th Division on the right had
taken Comiso and its airfield that day,
capturing 125 German planes (20 of
them in operating condition), 200,000
gallons of aviation gasoline, and 500
bombs. A rifle company, disregarding
the army boundary line, entered
Ragusa, captured the mayor and
chief of police, and seized the telephone switchboard; some Americans
' Italian descent amused themselves
by answering telephone calls from
anxious garrisons that wanted to
know what was going on. From
Licata, the 3rd Division had ballooned
out its original beach-head and held a
substantial amount of ground, troops
some cases cccupying positions
miles from Licata, around a broad
semicircle through Palma di Monte-
chiaro, Naro, and Campbello.

With firm contact between adjacent
units established all along the front,
with part of the 2nd Armoured Division
ashore and in action on the left, with
warships still on station to render
support, and with supplies and equipment moving ashore steadily, the
invasion appeared to be a success.

Yet Patton was far from ready to
rest on his laurels. He told Major-
General Terry de la Mesa Allen, the
1st Division commander, to get on
with taking Ponte Olivo and Niscemi,
which, according to the pre-invasion
plans, should have been secured that
day (11th July), the second day of the
landings.

Since Patton had expected the
severe enemy counterattacks that had
materialized, he had acted early that
morning to bolster the forces around
Gela, ordering an airborne regiment
to be dropped into the 1st Division
beach-head during the night of 11th
July. With that additional strength,
the Americans could take the next
objectives handily – the high ground
rimming the amphibious assault
beaches that would give the beach-
head protection and security.

The idea of reinforcing the beach-
head troops by means of an air drop
was excellent; no one suspected how
tragic the execution would be.

67

Airborne
reinforcement

Dropping paratroopers into a beach-head was about as quick a way of getting reinforcement as possible, and long before the invasion, Patton had asked Major-General Matthew B. Ridgway to look into the idea. The commander of the 82nd Airborne Division, Ridgway found the prospect eminently feasible. There was one danger – that Allied warships might fire on the planes carrying the para-troopers to the island. He therefore tried repeatedly to get assurances from the naval authorities that they would respect a cleared aerial corridor to Sicily. The naval commanders were reluctant to guarantee access of this sort, for planes appearing suddenly, particularly when flying at low altitudes, posed a menace to ships that they had to counter quickly. Naval anti-aircraft gunners, although trained in the identification of aircraft, had to be swift to reply to the threat.

Several days before the landings, Cunningham's representatives finally advised Ridgway that the naval forces would co-operate, but only if the aircraft strictly followed a designated route, with the last leg of the flight over land.

With that promise, Ridgway, together with staff personnel from air transport headquarters and from the naval command, worked out a specific course. Travelling along a corridor two miles wide and at an altitude of 1,000 feet, the planes were to reach Sicily at Sampieri, 30 miles east of Gela and at the extreme eastern end of the Seventh Army zone. They were then to proceed inland before turning northwest for the final leg over Sicily.

When Patton on 11th July asked that the operation be laid on, he indicated that he wanted the airborne troops to jump over the Gela-Farello airstrip, which was in American possession. This fitted in perfectly with the prior plan of having the planes hit Sampieri, then swing northwest for the final approach. The pilots would be flying over Allied territory all the way, without having to worry about enemy anti-aircraft fire.

At 8.45 am on 11th July, as soon as Patton received word from Ridgway that the troopers would jump that night, he sent messages to the naval command and to his principal sub-ordinate commanders. He informed them of the airborne drop and directed them to notify all their units, especially the anti-aircraft battalions, that American parachutists would be coming in shortly before midnight.

Ridgway, having started the necessary preparations in North Africa flew to Sicily that afternoon. He checked to make sure that the Seventh Army headquarters had disseminated the warning order to all anti-aircraft units, and then visited several anti-aircraft crews near the 1st Division command post to see whether they had received the information. Five crews, he discovered, had received the warning, but a sixth had not. When he brought this to the attention of a staff officer at army headquarters, he was informed that officers from all the anti-aircraft units in the vicinity were meeting late that afternoon to be briefed specifically on the airborne drop that night. The instructions to hold fire would be passed to everyone.

It so happened that the anti-aircraft gunners were having a busy day, for the Luftwaffe and Italian air force together launched almost 500 sorties against the Allied beach-head on 11th July, most of them in the Seventh Army area. A heavy air attack had struck beaches and ships at dawn. At 6.35 am 12 Italian planes swept over the transport area off the Gela shore and forced ships to weigh anchor, disperse, and take evasive action; two transports received near misses, one of them being badly damaged by a hole blown in its side. At 2 pm again four planes strafed the Gela beaches and a bomber at high altitude dropped five bombs on the anchorage area. Half an hour later, four bombers appeared over the Scoglitti area an a little after 3.30 pm 30 Junkers 88 attacked the Gela area; one bomb struck a Liberty ship loaded with ammunition, and the ship exploded and sank in shallow water. With both exposed and smoke pouring from the hulk, the destroyed ship served as a perfect beacon.

In Tunisia, Colonel Reuben H. Tucker's parachute infantry regiment of little more than 2,000 men took off at 7 pm in 144 aircraft. The pilots flew a basic nine-ship V of V's formation with each unit stepped down to enable pilots to see better the silhouette of the leading aircraft against the sky. The air was calm, and a quarter moon gave some illumination. The pilots were confident this would be a routine operation.

Following the prescribed course, the pilots rounded the corner at Malta and headed for Sicily with all formations intact. Some Allied ships north of Malta fired a few rounds of light anti-aircraft fire at the planes but without inflicting damage. Inside the aircraft, paratroopers dozed or sat quietly.

At 9.50 pm, while the planes were approaching Sicily, German aircraft in large numbers appeared over Gela and launched a massive attack. Allied planes joined the fray, and the dark sky over Gela became a dizzy kaleidoscope of Allied and Axis aircraft dodging among the explosions and the puffs of black anti-aircraft fire. Pandemonium reigned for almost an hour, as ships weighed anchor and dispersed to escape bombs.

The fighting aircraft had gone and the noise was dying down about the time the air transports bringing the paratroopers crossed the coastline near Sampieri. The leading flight flew peacefully to the Gela-Farello landing ground, and at 10.40 the first parachutists jumped; the second flight was in sight of Biviere Pond, the final checkpoint, when a single machine gun on the ground opened fire on the formation.

It was an American machine gun, and with minutes every Allied anti-aircraft gun in the beach-head and offshore, it seemed, was blasting the slow-flying, majestic columns of aircraft, knocking some planes out of the sky. Ridgway, waiting at the Gela-Farello landing ground to welcome the paratroopers, was thunderstruck – and furiously helpless.

Squadrons immediately broke apart, tried to form again, and scattered. Eight pilots swung back and returned to North Africa with their paratroopers but most dropped their human cargoes where they could, and some men inevitably fell into the sea. Six planes received direct hits as

Major-General Matthew B Ridgway

Above: LST burning after the German attacks on the invasion convoy, off Gela. *Below:* The price of failure

parachutists were trying to get out of the door to jump, some paratroopers were killed before they could get out, others were hit in their parachutes as they descended, and a few were shot after landing.

One pilot flew through heavy anti-aircraft fire and felt his plane shudder under the impact of a hit just as the paratroopers were bailing out of the door. No sooner had they jumped than the plane was struck again. With his rudder shot away, his engines sputtering and finally failing, the pilot crash-landed into the sea – at which an American destroyer fired on the downed craft for several seconds with 20-mm guns until the crews realized that the plane was American. The destroyer then sent a small boat to pick up the survivors.

Hysteria had swept the Gela area;

and when it was over and the losses were totalled, the results were tragic. Of the 144 planes that had departed Tunisia, 23 never returned – of which six had been shot down before the paratroopers could jump, and 37 were badly damaged. Altogether 229 casualties were sustained among the paratroopers – 82 dead, 131 wounded, and 16 missing. The airborne regiment had been scattered over a wide area, and most of the survivors would never forget – or forgive – the experience.

One pilot being debriefed ruefully said, 'Evidently the safest place for us tonight while over Sicily would have been over enemy territory.'

A full-scale investigation was ordered immediately, but it was inconclusive. The troop carrier command blamed the accident on the lack of co-ordination among the services – Army, Navy, and Air Forces, the American air forces commander placed the fault on the poor discipline of the anti-aircraft units, the Allied air force commander, Tedder, said that the mission had been improperly planned and was unsound because the planes had had to travel over 35 miles of battlefront. 'Even if it was physically possible for all the troops and ships to be duly warned, which is doubtful,' he said, 'any fire opened either by mistake or against any enemy aircraft would almost certainly be supported by all troops within range. AA firing at night is infectious and control almost impossible.' Cunningham blamed bad routing or faulty navigation by the aircraft crews. Some anti-aircraft units said they had never received the warning order, while others said that the air carriers had appeared while enemy planes were still aloft.

Ridgway seemed to sum up the matter best of all. 'The responsibility for loss of life and material resulting from this operation is so divided, so difficult to fix with impartial justice,' he wrote, 'that disciplinary action is of doubtful wisdom. Deplorable as is the loss of life which occurred, I believe that the lessons now learned . . . provide a sound basis for the belief that recurrences can be avoided.'

But this prediction, even after what had happened, would prove too optimistic.

The crack in the Axis alliance

The Fascist propaganda system had, by July 1943, become a victim of its own effluence, even to the extent of deluding Mussolini. So often had the theme of an impassioned defence of the homeland by the armed forces and civilians been repeated that most Italians expected efficiency and morale to improve when the war reached Italian soil. However indifferently Italian soldiers had fought overseas, they would react with firm and aggressive determination to repel invasion.

The initial bulletins after the invasion of Sicily confirmed this thesis. Optimistic reports followed by word of successful counterattacks prompted celebrations in Rome and elsewhere, and the fall of Pantelleria was forgotten in the exuberance.

The third daily release, issued on 12th July, was something else. While praising the resistance of the coastal units, extolling the excellent fighting qualities of the Livorno and Napoli Divisions, it conceded the Allied occupation of the coastline from Licata to Augusta and spoke of containing rather than eliminating the Allied beach-heads. Worst of all, the collapse of the naval base at Augusta-Syracuse was beyond comprehension to the Italian people and to Mussolini. This was the needle that pricked the expanding bubble of enthusiasm and new-born faith.

Hitler had no illusions. As early as the second day of the invasion, 11th July, he was firm in his conviction to reinforce the defenders of Sicily for reasons of his own. What concerned him most was his expectation of an Allied thrust into the Balkans, which he feared would be triggered by Allied conquest of Sicily. Hardly less important in his thinking, Sicily would give the Allies bomber bases closer to the industrial cities of northern Italy and to Germany. Since Hitler could hold Sicily and the Italian mainland as a bulwark against an assault on the Balkans only with Italian co-operation, his first course was to combat Italian discouragement. He knew that the Italians were tired of the war, and unless he bolstered them, they might withdraw from the conflict altogether.

He therefore told Kesselring to move the 1st Parachute Division by air from France to Sicily, to transfer the 29th Panzer Grenadier Division from Calabria across the Strait of Messina, and to shift the XIV Panzer Corps headquarters to the island to direct all the German units engaged.

Flying to Sicily on 12th July to co-ordinate these actions, Kesselring found Guzzoni and von Senger pessimistic about the prospect of repelling the Allied invasion – and Kesselring had to agree. All concerned had mixed feelings about the two new divisions about to come to the island, fearing that these additional troops would put a strain on transportation and supply facilities. Privately, von Senger was inclined to oppose the introduction of any more German units into Sicily because he believed that an immediate evacuation of the island was the best way to insure strong preparations for the defence of the Italian mainland.

It was clear to all three officers that further counterattacks against the Allied beach-heads could not be launched. Until the reinforcements arrived, the Axis would have to go over entirely to defence, and the only feasible course was to shorten the front to a line across the north-eastern corner of Sicily, move there by stages, delay the Allies to the extent possible, and hold out indefinitely – or until some decision, development, or sudden turn of events made another strategy possible.

The first thing to do, obviously, was to prevent a British break-through to Catania, which Schmalz had, thus far, done brilliantly. But Schmalz – his regiment helped by the battered Napoli Division was holding off far superior British forces – needed help, and Guzzoni had already ordered the Hermann Göring Division to move there, with the Livorno Division screening the area between that German division and the 15th Panzer Grenadier Division coming from the west.

After a frank and cordial discussion with Guzzoni, Kesselring and von Senger flew to Catania and talked with Schmalz, whom they complimented. Two separate infantry battalions had crossed the strait to reinforce him, and a parachute regiment was due to fly in that evening.

At 6 pm, while Kesselring waited to

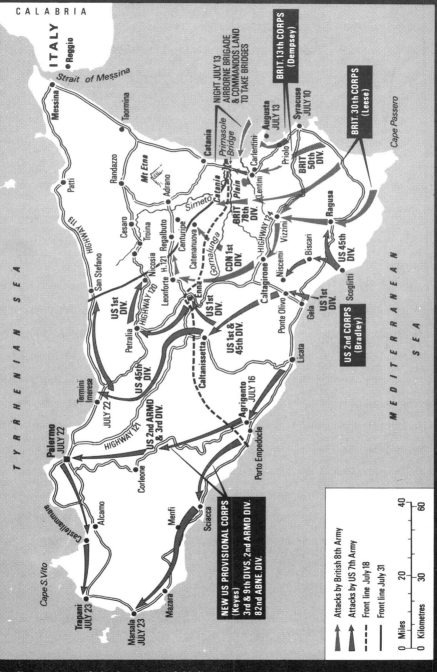

The first stages of the invasion of Sicily

take off to return to Rome, he watched a regiment of the 1st Parachute Division fly in under fighter plane escort and jump onto the Catania airfield. The operation went off without a hitch, and the paratroopers quickly boarded trucks to reinforce Group Schmalz.

Comando Supremo was deciding that evening of 12th July that it was impossible to repel the Allied landings. The coastal defences had collapsed, and Axis inferiority in naval and air strength permitted the Allies to land troops in Sicily faster than the Axis forces could augment their own units. Since the counterattacks had failed, the only effective defence was to wage war on the Allied sea lanes – against the Allied reinforcements being brought from North Africa to Sicily. Thus, the air forces defending Sicily had to be increased. Since Italy had no reserves in planes, Mussolini would have to ask Hitler for help.

This Ambrosio told Hitler on the morning of 13th July.

Kesselring at the same time was telephoning Colonel-General Alfred Jodl at OKW to report his impressions. He described the situation on the island as critical, emphasising that there was no chance to mount another concerted counterattack against the beach-heads. The best the Axis could do was to fight for time, which would be important if Italian morale was to be maintained and strengthened. He proposed that the remainder of the 1st Parachute Division and all of the 29th Panzer Grenadier Division be moved to Sicily, that the Luftwaffe be reinforced, and that submarines and motor boats operate more actively against Allied convoys.

Then Kesselring went to see Mussolini, who, he found, was shocked by the developments. Mussolini told him that he was asking Hitler for help, and in a telegram dispatched that day, Mussolini said he needed more planes immediately, but only for a short time. Once the crisis in Sicily was surmounted, he would return the aircraft. 'If we do not throw out the invaders right now', Mussolini told Hitler, 'it will be too late.'

By this time, OKW was discussing with Hitler the question of whether to reinforce the defence of Sicily. Jodl felt that in view of developments Sicily could not be held for long, so perhaps it would be better to renounce Sicily altogether in favour of preparing the defences of the Italian mainland and Germany. Hitler asked that Kesselring be consulted, and on the telephone, Kesselring recommended the continued defence of Sicily, mainly on the ground of bolstering Italian morale.

Hitler then decided to help Mussolini. He approved moving the rest of the 1st Parachute Division to Sicily; shifting the 29th Panzer Grenadier Division to the tip of Calabria for possible transfer to Sicily if enough supplies were available to support it; transferring Hube's XIV Panzer Corps headquarters to Sicily at once to take control of the German forces; and reinforcing the German Second Air Corps in Sicily and southern Italy. The task of the German troops in Sicily, he defined, was to 'delay the enemy advance as much as possible and to bring it to a halt in front of the Etna along a defensive line running approximately from San Stefano via Adrano to Catania.'

He also issued special instructions that were to be kept secret from the Italians. Hube was to exclude Guzzoni and other Italian command echelons from German planning. He was to assume the complete direction of operations in Sicily, extending his command to those Italian units still useful in combat.

Jodl enlarged on Hitler's secret orders. He told Hube to conduct the operations in Sicily in accordance with the aim of saving as many Germans as possible.

Kesselring informed Ambrosio on 14th July that the northeastern corner of Sicily, in the German view, was defensible and that Hube's XIV Panzer Corps headquarters would be transferred from southern Italy to the island. Hube would help Guzzoni hold the Etna Line by assuming command of the German forces.

On that day, Ambrosio saw Mussolini, told him there was no hope of winning the war, said there was no military justification for continuing fighting, and urged him to withdraw Italy from the conflict. He presented a formal memorandum to the Duce to

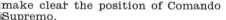
Left: Colonel-General Alfred Jodl.
Right: General Vittorio Ambrosio

make clear the position of Comando Supremo.

'The fate of Sicily,' Ambrosio had written, 'must be considered sealed within a more or less brief period. The essential reasons for the rapid collapse are: the absolute lack of naval opposition and the weak aerial opposition during the approach to the coast, the debarkation, the penetration of the adversary during our counter-offensive reactions; the inadequacy of the armament and of the distribution of our coastal divisions; the scarcity and lack of strength of our defensive works; the slight efficiency (armament and mobility) of the Italian reserve divisions. It is useless to search for the causes of this state of affairs: they are the result of three years of war begun with scanty means and during which the few resources have been burned up in Africa, in Russia, in the Balkans.'

Ambrosio concluded his appeal by asking 'the highest political authorities' – meaning Mussolini – 'to consider if it be not appropriate to spare the country further fighting and defeats, and to anticipate the end of the struggle, given that the final result will un-

doubtedly be worse within one or a few years.'

The military wanted Mussolini to have a showdown with Hitler, withdraw from the alliance, and make peace with the Allies.

Mussolini said he would give the matter some thought.

Hitler's military advisers at OKW also hoped for a showdown. They were disenchanted with what they considered the feeble Italian resistance in Sicily, the ineptitude of Mussolini's government, the perpetual bickering with Comando Supremo. On 14th July they brought up to date plans they had had on hand for some time – if Mussolini and his government collapsed or sought a way out of the war, German troops would move into northern Italy in strength and occupy that part of the country.

The invasion of Sicily, then, in the first days produced a crack in the Italo-German alliance, and that fissure exposed the pitiful weakness of the Italian state.

The campaign develops

Montgomery was pleased with the results of the first two days of the invasion, even though the weather and the mountainous character of Sicily were exhausting his troops more quickly than he had anticipated. Temperatures were high during the day, water was short, the roads were extremely dusty, and everywhere were hills that had to be climbed. Already there was evidence that the soldiers were tiring.

But they were in no worse condition than the enemy, and this was no time to relax. He pushed his two corps commanders on.

The XIII Corps had some trouble proceeding beyond Syracuse on 12th July and had to go over temporarily to defence when Group Schmalz and the Napoli Division launched a rather severe counterattack. Actually the counterattack was undertaken to cover a withdrawal to good defensive positions centered on Lentini, for lacking sufficient resources to establish a solid defensive line in depth forward of Lentini, Schmalz struck quickly, then pulled back. When he retired, he uncovered Augusta. The British having beaten off the counterattack with the help of air and naval forces, moved forward as the enemy pressure slackened; that night the 5th Division entered the port city of Augusta. With that, Montgomery felt that the Allies firmly held the southeastern portion of the island.

On 13th July Dempsey's XIII Corps came up against the Lentini positions on the coastal road to Catania and bounced off.

Recognizing the strength of Schmalz's defences, Montgomery looked to his left and to the XXX Corps for progress. If he could get Leese's troops quickly to Caltagirone, Enna, and Leonforte, he could swing around the western side of Mount Etna and get behind the enemy troops blocking access to Catania in the east. There was one problem. Highway 124, which offered the quickest way of getting into the interior and around Mount Etna, was, according to Alexander's pre-invasion instructions, reserved for use by the Americans.

Montgomery simply ignored Alexander's directions. He told Leese to attack along the highway and by so doing, he violated the army boundary, denied the Americans a road they were counting on using, and, worst of all, sent the XXX Corps directly across the right part of the Seventh Army line of advance. The result of this arrogant act probably prolonged the campaign.

Later, Montgomery explained his action by writing: 'There was a danger of overlapping between the two armies in the area Vizzini – Caltagirone, but this was put right by orders from Alexander's 15th Army Group which made the road . . . inclusive to Eighth Army' – which was less than a full and frank explanation.

The chain of events leading to the highhandedness started on 12th July when Patton, like Montgomery, was cheerful over the course of the invasion and optimistic over future prospects. The 1st Division had taken the Ponte Olivo airfield, hurting the Livorno Division still more in the process; the 45th Division had captured Biscari; and the 3rd Division was in firm possession of Licata, which anchored the left flank.

Beyond this, Patton had no specific instructions from Alexander on the next phase of operations. His army had taken the assigned objectives, and his troops were in a firm position, as Alexander had directed, 'to prevent enemy reserves moving eastwards against the left flank of Eighth Army'– but since he was naturally aggressive and was averse to standing idly by, he told Major-General Truscott to launch a reconnaissance in force – less than a full-scale attack – with his 3rd Division along the coast to Agrigento. He also instructed Bradley to keep advancing the 1st and 45th Divisions inland, generally toward Caltagirone.

Alexander visited Patton on the morning of 13th July and approved his actions. Patton explained that if he could take Agrigento and its satellite harbour, Porto Empedocle, he would ease his logistical problems; and he also pointed out that Bradley's II Corps, by taking Caltagirone, Enna, and Leonforte, might prevent the 15th Panzer Grenadier Division from linking up with the Hermann Göring Division, which was obviously moving to strengthen the block against Montgomery in front of Catania. Then

ft: Lieutenant-General Sir Miles
empsey. Right: Lieutenant-General
r Oliver Leese

rhaps, Bradley could swing around
e western slope of Mount Etna to
andazzo and beyond in order to pro-
de a drive that would complement
ontgomery's advance through
tania to Messina.

Alexander seemed to agree. Specific-
ly, he said it was all right to take
grigento if Patton could do so with
tle expenditure of manpower or
aterial, but he preferred, he said, to
ep the 3rd Division on the left as a
lid wall against the sizeable enemy
ovements from the west – meaning
e 15th Panzer Grenadier Division –
at reconnaissance pilots were re-
rting.

Leaving Patton, Alexander visited
ontgomery, who persuaded him to
ake the boundary change that
uld give him Highway 124.

The 45th Division on the Seventh
my right, while taking Niscemi, was
ready rubbing up against the Eighth
my's XXX Corps which was moving

Major-General Lucian K Truscott

into positions to start Montgomery's new attack, and Major-General Troy H. Middleton, the 45th Division commander, feared that the close proximity of his troops to the British who were shifting over, might provoke accidental exchanges of fire. As it happened, even before Alexander acceded to Montgomery's request, the latter had issued orders for a major attack to start that evening.

Several hours after Montgomery's attack started, Alexander radioed a directive to Patton confirming the validity of Montgomery activities, so that it was just before midnight of 13th July when Patton received the message. He was to hand Highway 124 over to Montgomery.

But the message also meant that the Seventh Army was to have a passive role in the campaign. Montgomery was to get all the roads leading to Messina, the prize of the Sicily campaign.

Patton took his medicine like a man. He phoned Bradley and informed him that giving up Highway 124 would re-

quire sideslipping the 45th Division the west and around the other side the 1st Division, while the II Corp instead of advancing to the nort would have to turn to the west.

'This will raise hell with us,' Bradl said. 'I had counted heavily on t road.'

That was too bad. What was wor was that moving the 45th Divisi took the pressure off the Herma Göring Division, which was shifti over to contest Montgomery at t entrance to the Catania plain. It al allowed the 15th Panzer Grenadi Division, which was travelling fro the western part of the island to t centre and which was getting snagg on tentacles extended around Lica by the US 3rd Division, to make fir link-up with the Hermann Göri Division. Had Bradley been able maintain his pressure, the Alli might have driven into a gap cover only by the shattered remnants of t Livorno Division, thus perhaps pr venting the two German divisions the two strongest units in Sicily from erecting a solid defensive li around Mount Etna.

Montgomery's major attack, scheduled for the night of 13th July, was an attempt to break into the Catania Plain from the Lentini area. To help force the bottleneck between Carlenni and Lentini, he planned to have a parachute brigade land from the sky during the night and a Commando unit land from the sea to seize two important bridges, the former taking the Primasole bridge across the Simeto river 7 miles south of Catania, the latter, after coming ashore near Agnoe, taking the Lentini bridge. With heavy naval support, the 50th Division with an armoured brigade in the lead, was to make the chief thrust to link up with the Commando and airborne troops.

Soon after darkness on the night of 13th July Commando units landed and seized the Lentini bridge. The Germans had placed demolitions along the structure as a precautionary measure in the event they were forced to withdraw, intending to explode the dynamite charges and deny the use of the bridge to the British. The Commandos removed the explosive charges from the structure and set up defences round the bridge, but they were unable to hold. A strong contingent of German troops soon appeared and drove off the lightly armed British raiders.

The airborne operation, a more complicated venture, ran into the same difficulties as the previous ones. The troop-carrier pilots encountered heavy anti-aircraft fire from Allied ships along the eastern shore of Sicily even though a specifically designated route was supposed to have been cleared of shipping – and in fact from the time the aircraft rounded Malta, they were under anti-aircraft fire. Off Cape Passero, they ran into real trouble. More than half the pilots reported receiving hits from Allied naval craft, two aircraft were actually shot down and nine turned back after pilots were injured or planes were damaged.

And those planes continuing on course ran into a solid wall of anti-aircraft shells from German and Italian batteries once they crossed the coastline. Many pilots fell out of formation and circled while trying to find a way through the fire to the four drop zones, and ten more aircraft turned back, each with a full load of British paratroopers.

Of the 108 planes that had started, 87 threaded their way through the fire – but only 39 dropped their parachutists within a mile or so of the drop zones, most of the other paratroopers coming to earth 10 miles away from the Primasole bridge, and some were as far as the slopes of Mount Etna, 20 miles distant.

Of the 1,900 members of the British Parachute Brigade who were despatched to Sicily, only about 200 men and three anti-tank guns reached the Primasole bridge and seized it. They promptly removed the German demolition charges and set up a perimeter defence, but they constituted a pitifully small force to hold out until the ground forces arrived overland.

By coincidence, the bridge was near the Catania airfield where the regiment of the German 1st Parachute Division – the first contingent of the division to arrive in Sicily – had dropped a few hours earlier as Kesselring had watched. The German paratroopers reacted savagely to the intrusion of the British paratroopers, and a fierce battle that started at daylight of 14th July lasted all day. At nightfall, having hung on despite heavy losses, the surviving British withdrew from the bridge to a piece of high ground overlooking the structure, and from there they covered the bridge by fire and at least prevented the Germans from damaging it.

Meanwhile, the attack by the 50th Division had made little progress, for Schmalz was now reinforced not only by paratroopers, but by two independent infantry battalions ferried over the Messina strait. During the afternoon of 14th July when some British tanks finally worked their way into the German defensive line, Schmalz, who was apprehensive of being outflanked and cut off from a withdrawal route, decided to leave the Lentini positions and fall back. Behind small delaying forces, Schmalz pulled back his troops in two steps, first eight miles to the northern bank of the Gornalunga river, then early on 15th July three miles farther behind the Simeto river.

As the Germans withdrew, the

Above: Self-propelled 105mm 'Priests' moving up to the front.
Below: The crew of a 6 pounder anti-tank gun cover the roads on the outskirts of a village

British moved forward and joined the paratroopers still holding out at the southern end of the Primasole bridge. A thrust north of the river on 15th July netted no ground, for the bulk of the Hermann Göring Division was arriving to strengthen Schmalz's defences, but on 16th July a heavier British attack gained a shallow bridgehead across the Simeto. On the following day, the British extended the bridgehead to a depth of 3,000 yards. An attack during the night of 17th July failed to make any headway.

It became obvious that the defensive line covering Catania was too strong to be broken, at least for the moment. Montgomery's effort to reach Messina up the east coast road was stymied.

Alexander's directive of 13th July having excluded Patton from participating in the capture of Messina, and thereby limited the Seventh Army to a passive role in the campaign, the Seventh Army commander cast his eyes on Palermo, the largest city in Sicily. If he was to be denied any part of Messina, perhaps he could gain all of Palermo – and the first step toward Palermo would be the capture of Agrigento and Porto Empedocle; since Alexander had authorized a reconnaissance in force to those objectives, Patton told Truscott to go ahead. Agrigento represented the gateway to western Sicily, and Porto Empedocle would augment the minor harbour capacities of Gela and Licata.

While Truscott struck out for Agrigento, 25 miles from Licata, Patton set about drawing up his own plans for the reduction of Sicily. He established two corps zones for his army, one for Bradley's II Corps, the other for a new Provisional Corps headed by his deputy army commander, Major-General Geoffrey T. Keyes, and he extended the boundary line between the two forces to the northern coast of Sicily. East of the line, Bradley was to have the 1st and 45th Divisions. When the 45th shifted from its position on the right of the 1st Division to the left, the two divisions were to drive to the northwest toward Caltanissetta, then continue to the northern coast and split the island in two. Keyes was to have the 3rd Division after it took Agrigento, the 82nd Airborne Division, and that part of the 9th Division that had come ashore after the invasion. The 2nd Armoured Division in army reserve was to be ready to exploit any offensive opportunity, possibly in the western portion of Sicily where the ground is less mountainous, most likely in the final drive to Palermo.

By the early afternoon of 16th July Truscott's forces had encircled Agrigento and silenced all the Italian artillery. Fires were burning in many places in the city, and when American troops broke through the outer defences and reached the city streets, the Italian commander surrendered. Porto Empedocle had already fallen to the Rangers.

On that day, Alexander published a new directive modifying the orders he had issued three days earlier. Montgomery was definitely to drive to

Messina while Patton protected his flank by advancing to the north coast of Sicily on the British left. Alexander authorised the seizure of Agrigento and Porto Empedocle, which were already in American possession. He said nothing about Palermo.

Having accepted the earlier directive without comment or complaint, Patton now became angry at what he considered a distinct slap at the capabilities of his army. To guard Montgomery's rear was hardly commensurate with the concept of equal partnership with opportunities and honours to be shared by American and British forces. Conferring with his closest advisers, he discovered that there was widespread indignation among American commanders over the role assigned in the campaign to the Seventh Army.

As Bradley said, the Seventh Army was to be confined to the western half of the island where 'there was little to be gained' and 'there was no glory in the capture of hills, docile peasants, and spiritless soldiers.' After reaching the northern coast, 'we can sit comfortably on our prats while Monty finishes the goddam war.' What the Americans wanted was a shot at Messina. But denied that, they would accept Palermo.

Patton decided to protest. He did so by asking to meet Alexander in North Africa for the purpose of presenting an alternative plan.

On 17th July meeting with Alexander at La Marsa, Tunisia, Patton requested permission to take Palermo. After considerable discussion, Alexander agreed, and returning exuberantly to Sicily, Patton issued a directive spelling out Palermo as the main Seventh Army objective. He wanted Bradley to strike to the northern coast of Sicily with the 1st Division, while the 45th Division angled to the northwest directly on Palermo, with, on the left, Keyes' Provisional Corps with the 82nd Airborne and 3rd Divisions moving on Palermo from the south and southwest. He expected to use the 2nd Armoured Division for the final thrust into the city.

American intelligence officers believed that the Italians who comprised the great bulk of the enemy troops in the western portion of Sicily were capable of only limited defensive action. They were right, for when Guzzoni learned of the fall of Agrigento, he realised that he would have to move the XII Italian Corps from the west to the east or probably lose these troops. Since the major Axis effort was to be made in the northeastern corner of the island, he ordered Zingales on 17th July to move his headquarters and the Aosta and Assietta Divisions eastwards to Nicosia, leaving two coastal divisions to ward off possible Allied amphibious attacks on the western coast. To defend Palermo, Guzzoni named Generale di Divisione Giovanni Marciani to take charge of all coastal units. This would leave little more than 60,000 troops in the western part of Sicily, including units at the Palermo and Marsala naval bases; but they were, for the most part, second rate – badly equipped and poorly trained.

Four hours after Patton ordered the advance to Palermo, the Seventh Army headquarters received Alexander's written confirmation of approval; but Patton's chief of staff, Brigadier-General Hobart L. Gay, who saw the message first, was somewhat shocked by the contents. Instead of giving Patton a free hand, Alexander imposed certain restrictions – conditions he had not indicated to Patton during their conference – ordering Patton to advance to the north coast – in order to guarantee strong protection to the Eighth Army flank and rear before setting out for Palermo.

Outraged, Gay practised some sleight of hand. He used the first part of Alexander's message to modify slightly Bradley's mission, but he ignored the rest. He made certain that decoding procedures were delayed, then pretending that the original had been garbled in transmission, he asked the army group headquarters to send another message. By the time the message had been repeated, the Seventh Army had troops on the outskirts of Palermo.

The reason for Alexander's modified directive stemmed from Montgomery's growing realization that he lacked the strength to encircle Mount Etna and break into Catania at the me time. When the XIII Corps drive the east coast of Sicily stalled at the Simento river, Montgomery ordered the XXX Corps on the left to push 'with all speed' into the interior. But it soon became apparent that Leese would have to shorten the arc of his encirclement, and as he narrowed the attack and shifted his forces somewhat to the right, he left Enna open. Bradley, after co-ordinating with Leese, took Enna with the 1st Division, then turned his forces northeast to protect the British flank, thus leaving the task of cutting Sicily in two to the 45th Division, which was ready to go the 80 miles to the northern shore on the afternoon of 18th July. The Provisional Corps was ready to go for Palermo on the following morning.

The American advances turned out to be little more than a vast road march. Reconnaissance troops screening the main bodies of troops brushed aside a few opposing Italians, for

Right: General Bradley.
Below: On to Palermo! The mobility of Patton's army was astonishing

Top left: A conflict of civilisation.
Left: Villagers admire a 6.1 inch rifle.
Top Centre: Italian resistance in the
West was easily overcome. *Above:* US
mounted howitzer in action outside
Palermo

several rounds of cannon fire were usually enough to convince Italian defenders of roadblocks or bridges that they had no chance of stalling the American movement.

On the morning of 22nd July the 45th Division was striking for the northern shore about 30 miles east of Palermo, while the 3rd Division and part of the 2nd Armoured Division were moving directly toward the port city. Late that afternoon the 45th Division reached the coast near Termini Imerese, and the two others were at the outskirts of Palermo and ready to launch an assault. But the garrison and civilian population had had

enough of the war and were happy to give up. Because General Marciani, commander of the Italian defensive forces, had been taken prisoner, the ceremonial act fell to Generale di Brigata Guiseppe Molinere, who offered his capitulation to Keyes shortly after being picked up by a patrol which entered the city late in the afternoon. Around 7 pm, on the steps of the royal palace, Keyes formally accepted the surrender.

On the following day, Americans mopped up the isolated ports in the west – Trapani, Marsala, and Castellammare.

Strategically, the capture of west-

US Seventh Army enters Palermo

ern Sicily was virtually meaningless. Yet it was a spectacular achievement that had important benefits, for at a cost of 272 battle casualties – 57 killed, 170 wounded and 45 missing – the Americans had taken 53,000 prisoners – though mostly reservists, militia, and uniformed policemen. They had also gained the port of Palermo, which would become the main entry point of supplies for the Seventh Army, although the original assault beaches, more than 100 miles away, would continue to operate.

The most important result perhaps was the demonstration of American tactical power and mobility. The prac-tice of having infantrymen ride tanks to battle became standard procedure and ranging far and wide, thrusting forward aggressively, the Seventh Army troops had shown balance and maturity. The only major problem was attacks by Allied aircraft on American tanks – the pilots thought the vehicles belonged to the 15th Pan-zer Grenadier Division, which had moved to the centre of the island to stabilize the Etna Line.

The American ground forces in their western drive captured the headlines at home, and they impressed Alexan-der who was now ready to give Patton a larger piece of the main action.

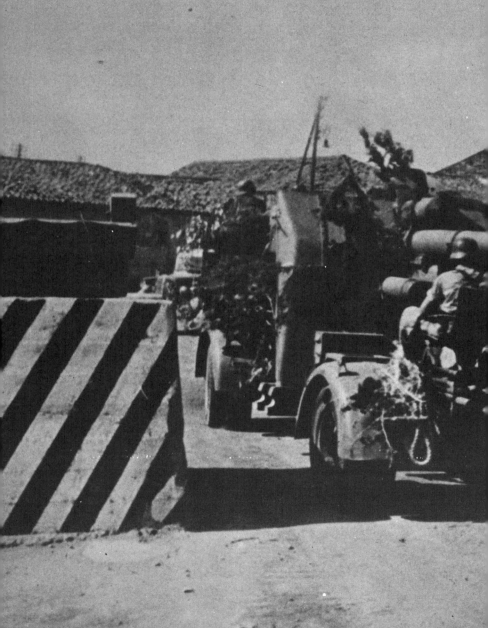

Above: Führer and Duce at Feltre, on 19th July. *Below:* Colonel-General Hans Hube

On 15th July when Hube and his XIV Panzer Corps headquarters arrived in Sicily to take charge of all the German forces on the island, Kesselring reminded Baade of the importance of his ferry service at Messina. Whether the Germans succeeded in reinforcing the troops in Sicily or in evacuating them – the course of action would be dictated by Hitler's decision – would depend in large measure on Baade's ability to keep the boats moving regularly – and Baade ran a cold and efficient, machine-like service entirely apart from the operation conducted by Italian military authorities.

The Italians were far more humane in their conduct of ferries. They were often willing to grant passage to or from Sicily to military personnel on leave and even civilians – for the most obscure reasons and on the most transparently flimsy excuses. They often overloaded their boats, and their engines, timetables, and intentions were constantly breaking down.

Before Hube took formal control of a sector of the front, he, Kesselring, and Guzzoni spent the better part of two days discussing the situation and a variety of plans. Guzzoni's concept of holding the Etna Line made sense, and Kesselring promised to send more troops to Sicily to help him defend it; all three officers agreeing that it was better to hold Sicily than to abandon it.

Guzzoni gave Hube responsibility for the eastern portion of the Etna Line, the important and constantly threatened Catania sector. He retained Zingales' XII Corps, now returned from the western part of the island, in the northern half, placing Rossi's XVI Corps headquarters in the northeastern corner of the island to receive and process units coming from the mainland – the 29th Panzer Grenadier Division was expected to arrive as soon as sufficient supplies were amassed to support it. On 18th July Hube assumed command of his area and control of the Hermann Göring, 15th Panzer Grenadier, and Livorno Divisions.

In contrast with these command arrangements in Sicily undertaken in a spirit of cordiality and good will, Hitler cynically admitted to a group of high-ranking military officers on 17th July that Sicily could not be held indefinitely. He wanted no units on the island denied supplies or support, but he wished OKW to be aware of the fact that ultimately all troops would have to be withdrawn. For the moment, he desired to postpone the movement of the 29th Panzer Grenadier Division to Sicily; for in a broader perspective, the shakiness of the Mussolini government made it necessary always to keep in mind, and consider the possibility and the results of, eventual Italian collapse. If that occurred, the Germans would have to take over the defence of Italy – but Hitler believed that the Germans would then have to pull back to a shorter line in Italy, somewhere in the north. For 'without the Italian army,' he said, 'we cannot hold the entire Italian peninsula.'

On the other hand, if there were no political collapse, if he had Mussolini's full support, Hitler could defend the whole of Italy.

A message from Mussolini on the following day clarified the issues. In a long telegram that made his position quite clear, the Duce frightened the Führer.

'The sacrifice of my country,' Mussolini had written, 'cannot have as its principal purpose that of delaying a direct attack on Germany. Germany is stronger economically and militarily than Italy. My country, which entered the war three years earlier than was foreseen and after it already had engaged in two wars, has step by step exhausted itself, burning up its resources in Africa, Russia, and the Balkans. I believe, Führer, that the time has come for us to examine the situation together attentively, in order to draw from it the consequences conforming to our common interests and to those of each of our countries.'

Putting aside his fears of being poisoned if he left Germany, Hitler immediately agreed to meet Mussolini somewhere in Italy in order to put him back on the track. He prepared to treat Mussolini with deference, to infuse him with faith in ultimate Axis victory, and to offer whatever was possible in the way of German reinforcement.

The dictators met in northern Italy, at Feltre, on 19th July. Ambrosio and Comando Supremo hoped that Mussolini would stand up to Hitler and make an end to the alliance – but they were disappointed. The conference consisted mainly of a harangue by Hitler that lasted several hours and left everyone but himself exhausted, his chief point being that the decisive battle should be fought in Sicily rather than in Italy. And to this end, he promised to send more troops, specifically the 29th Panzer Grenadier Division, which he was authorizing to be dispatched to Sicily that day.

While the heads of government were at Feltre, they received the ominous news that 500 Allied heavy bombers were attacking the railroad yards in Rome. This was the first time that the Allies had dared to bomb the Italian capital. and on his return there, Mussolini summoned Ambrosio on 20th July and told him he had decided to write a letter to Hitler to terminate the alliance.

Believing Mussolini incapable of confronting the Führer, Ambrosio spoke sharply, asked why Mussolini had not told Hitler so personally at Feltre, and offered his resignation, but the Duce refused to accept it and dismissed Ambrosio from the room.

Ambrosio and Comando Supremo then held a series of conferences. They decided on 21st July that since it was probably too much to expect Mussolini to break the alliance with Germany, they had no alternative but to fight to the limit in Sicily and they therefore asked OKW for two more German divisions. OKW replied that the 29th Panzer Grenadier Division was being sent across the Messina strait as fast as transportation permitted and that another division would follow in the near future.

As portions of the 29th Panzer Grenadier Division reached Sicily, Hube placed them in the line contiguous to the north coast. As a result, he had dependable German troops all along the front, and since German units were now the mainstay of the defence as the Italian forces had lost most of their combat effectiveness, Hube informed Guzzoni that he wanted to extend his tactical control to all the ground forces in Sicily – Italian as well as German.

Guzzoni refused. Handing over control to the Germans would be a sharp blow to Italian prestige, but more to the point, Guzzoni suspected that Hube had no intention of ever mounting a major counterattack. Without going over to the offensive, the Axis, no matter how long the northeastern corner of Sicily was held, would be unable to win the campaign.

Believing that the Allies would invade the Italian mainland, but only after they conquered Sicily, Guzzoni saw his duty as the task of postponing as long as possible the Allied conquest of Sicily. If he received substantial reinforcement, he might even return to the offensive and inflict a severe setback, if not an overwhelming defeat, on the Allies, and this would delay an invasion of the Italian mainland for some time. If he could even hold out in Sicily until the autumn months, the winter weather might make an invasion of Italy impossible until the following spring. This was well worth fighting for.

The idea was attractive, but it could be only a dream. Axis aircraft were no longer operating from Sicilian airfields – all had been withdrawn to the mainland, while in contrast Allied fighter-bombers and light bombers ha[d] taken possession of at least six excel[lent] landing grounds in Sicily. Fur[ther]more, except around Messina task forces of American and Britis[h] warships were off the shores of Sicil[y] and could neither be challenged no[r] dislodged.

When it became painfully evident t[o] Guzzoni that Comando Supremo, des[pite] its professed intention, was send[ing] no Italian reinforcements t[o] Sicily, he bowed to the facts; in vie[w] of the preponderance of Germa[n] strength, he agreed to let Hube con[duct] the actual land battle eve[n] though he, Guzzoni, retained nomina[l] overall command.

Hube was considerate. Taking tac[tical] control, he continued to discus[s] his plans and decisions with Guzzon[i] directly or through von Senger, th[e] German liaison officer to Guzzoni['s] headquarters, and although Hub[e] tried to maintain the impression tha[t] the Germans intended to fight bitterl[y] to the end in Sicily, he did not deceiv[e] Guzzoni. Powerless, Guzzoni sai[d] nothing.

The real German mission entruste[d] to Hube was to launch no major coun[terattack, to gain time, to execute a[n] orderly withdrawal from the island, an[d] to save German manpower for futur[e] battles expected to take place on th[e] Italian mainland.

The only question still open was th[e] matter of timing. So long as Mussolin[i] remained tied to Hitler, so long a[s] Italy maintained the alliance, so lon[g] as the appearance of unity prevailed[,] Hitler would do nothing to embarras[s] Mussolini or to turn the Italian[s] overtly against the Germans. But ho[w] long Mussolini could retain his politi[ca]l power was a matter of conjectur[e] and serious concern. The Italians[,] Hitler believed, were capable not onl[y] of defection but of treachery and i[f] they made a deal with the Allies an[d] turned on the Germans, they migh[t] isolate and imperil the considerab[le] German forces in Sicily and souther[n] Italy. With German manpower in ver[y] short supply, particularly after th[e] enormous losses at Stalingrad and th[e] even greater losses in Tunisia, Hitle[r] could ill afford to be anything but mos[t] careful in his military diplomacy.

Above: German troops mark occupied territory for the Luftwaffe. *Below:* A
Spitfire being serviced on a newly-captured Sicilian airfield

Allied changes

The ease with which they invaded Sicily surprised the Allied leaders and caught them unprepared to exploit immediately the relative Axis weakness.

On the last day of June, ten days before the landings, when Eisenhower had summed up his strategic thinking for the Combined Chiefs, he had said that he would be governed in his choice of the operations he believed ought to be undertaken beyond Sicily, by how the opening phases of the Sicily campaign went. For the enemy reaction would be one of the principal determinants in his recommendation. If the invasion of Sicily failed to bring Italy to surrender, he saw two alternatives: assault the 'toe' of the mainland, or invade Sardinia – and the basis for his selection of the more appropriate operation would be the strength and location of the German forces and the morale of the Italian Army. If effective and prolonged Axis resistance seemed unlikely, he would probably favour moving to the mainland; otherwise, he would be inclined toward Sardinia.

On 9th July (the day before the invasion of Sicily), plagued by the doubt that is a normal concomitant of a commander's loneliness on the eve of a risky operation, he expected his forces to meet strong opposition on the island. He informed Marshall that 'our resources' for post-Sicily operations were 'very slender indeed.'

Reality was quite a relief. Losses in shipping and landing craft – the prime factors in strategic planning for the Mediterranean theatre – were negligible, and the Italian forces appeared to be melting away. Even the Germans were reinforcing their troops on the island to a lesser extent than the Allies had anticipated.

Marshall consequently suggested to the Combined Chiefs of Staff on 16th July that they ought to consider seriously the prospect of invading the mainland of Italy. In order to bypass the mountainous terrain in the 'toe', he thought it might be possible to land farther up the 'boot' – say, in the Naples area; for if the Sicily campaign ended early enough, landings near Naples could be launched before the onset of winter weather, which would imperil unloading operations across

the beaches.

The Combined Chiefs were impressed, and they asked Eisenhower whether he believed that an invasion somewhere around Naples was feasible.

Eisenhower felt that the risks were too great. Shipping in the theatre was still in short supply, and single-engine fighter planes based on Sicilian airfields would, at Naples, be at the limit of or beyond their effective operating range. He preferred to land on the 'toe', just across the Strait of Messina, and on 18th July he asked approval from the Combined Chiefs to carry the war to the mainland in that way. Two days later, the Combined Chiefs approved his request, but added a rider reminding Eisenhower that he should keep in mind the advantages of invading Italy farther north.

Three days later still, on 23rd July, they were more categorical. While not actually instructing him to go ahead and execute landings, they directed Eisenhower to prepare a plan for a direct attack on Naples, for they had not yet reached a firm decision on post-Sicily possibilities. They ruled out neither Sardinia nor the 'toe'; but they wanted Eisenhower to be ready, should the opportunity arise, to go directly into Naples, thereby avoiding the difficult terrain of Calabria in the lower part of the Italian 'boot'. A direct movement into Naples would also gain that major port and the important nearby airfields quickly.

The rapidity with which Patton overran the western part of the island gave credence to the prevalent optimism that the campaign would end quickly in Sicily. This led to talk in Algiers of invading the mainland of Italy by what was called an ad hoc landing – an impromptu or improvised operation across the Messina strait even before all of Sicily was conquered – but although preliminary planning along these lines was undertaken, Montgomery saw the situation in quite different fashion. He tended to be pessimistic about a quick end to the campaign. He had brought three divisions up to force a passage to

Catania, and even the pressure exerted by the 5th, 50th, and 51st Divisions could make no headway along the east coast road against the strong defences of the Hermann Göring Division. On the Eighth Army left, the 1st Canadian Division was advancing against Leonforte to try to get around the western side of Mount Etna, and that thrust was going slowly against rugged terrain and stubborn opposition.

The topography of the island, Montgomery was well aware, favoured the Germans, who had organized a series of very strong positions to block access to Messina. In the steep-sided valleys and trackless hills, there was no effective way to mass and bring to bear the superiority the Allies enjoyed in tanks and artillery, and the war there had become a host of small-unit engagements, with infantrymen battling under an intensely hot sun.

Expecting no sudden breakthrough of the German defences, anticipating no swift German collapse, Montgomery was impressed by the strength of the forces opposing the Allies. The 29th Panzer Grenadier Division was in the north, the 15th Panzer Grenadier Division in the centre, the Hermann Göring Division in the east, and the 1st Parachute Division provided units bolstering key points, while the remnants of four Italian divisions – the Aosta and Assietta Divisions had joined the Livorno and Napoli Divisions in the Messina corner – were available to cover gaps, screen counterattacking thrusts, offer delaying action, and give general support.

Recognizing that he was unable to mount and launch two thrusts around Mount Etna strong enough to overcome the opposition, Montgomery called for the 78th Division to be brought from Sousse, Tunisia. He decided to shift his main effort from the right to the left. As soon as the 78th Division arrived in Sicily and took part of the front – he expected this to occur on August 1st – he would launch another major effort to reach Messina. In the meantime, his units on the right were to revert to an aggressive-defensive posture and the Canadians were to push toward Adrano, which Montgomery conceived was the key to the German Etna Line.

Upon this admission by Montgomery

of his inability to take Messina with out help, Alexander brought Patt into the picture by means of a dire tive he issued on 20th July. Once th Seventh Army reached the nor coast of the island, Patton was to se strong reconnaissance patrols ea ward along the two main east-we highways in the northern portion Sicily – Highway 113 along the coa Highway 120 some 20 miles inlan This would stretch the Germ defences and, more important, pr tect the Eighth Army flank.

Three days later, when the Seven Army had reached the northern sho and taken Palermo, Alexander cha ged his instructions. He now to Patton to use the maximum streng he could bring to bear on the two roa thus placing the Seventh Army equal footing with the Eighth Arm insofar as getting to Messina was co cerned. The significant strategic o jective on the island, the port city Messina, was now up for grabs.

Since the 2nd Armoured Divisi would be less useful in the troubl terrain of the northeastern corner Sicily, and since the 82nd Airborne a 45th Divisions had been selected f post-Sicily operations and would so have to be pulled out to prepare f them, whatever they might be, Patt called for the rest of the 9th Divisi to be sent from North Africa.

Meanwhile, the 45th Division hu ried eastward from Termini Imere along the coastal highway and car abreast of the 1st Division, whi Bradley had turned east along t inland road.

Two days later, on 25th July, t principal Allied ground commander Alexander, Montgomery, and Patto met at Cassibile to determine how be to finish off the Germans – the Italia were no longer regarded as effective and expel them from Sicily. The pl they formulated underscored t equality of the two armies. Patt was to continue eastward along t two roads assigned to him in 'a su tained relentless drive until the enem is decisively defeated.' Bradley wou continue to control the ground oper tions along these highways, and planned to relieve the 45th with t 3rd Division somewhere around t end of July and to replace the 1

The Goums were French colonial troops known for their skill with knives

Division with the 9th, as soon as the latter arrived in sufficient numbers to take over – probably in early August. Despite the scheduled changes, the Americans would continue to push hard.

Montgomery would make his major effort on the left with the 78th Division, after it arrived in Sicily, thrusting northward from Centuripe to Adrano, while the 1st Canadian Division advanced along Highway 121 through Regalbuto. Meanwhile, the XIII Corps on the right was to feint an attack toward Catania to deceive the Germans into thinking that this was the main British attack. After Adrano fell to British troops, Montgomery expected the Germans to pull out of Catania.

At the same time, British naval forces along the eastern coast were completing preparations for an amphibious end-run around Catania in order to get troops into Messina quickly. Perhaps the British could cut off and trap a considerable part of the withdrawing enemy forces. This would be a bonus.

While the Allied commanders were thus laying their plans on the sixteenth day of the invasion of Sicily, momentous events were taking place in Rome.

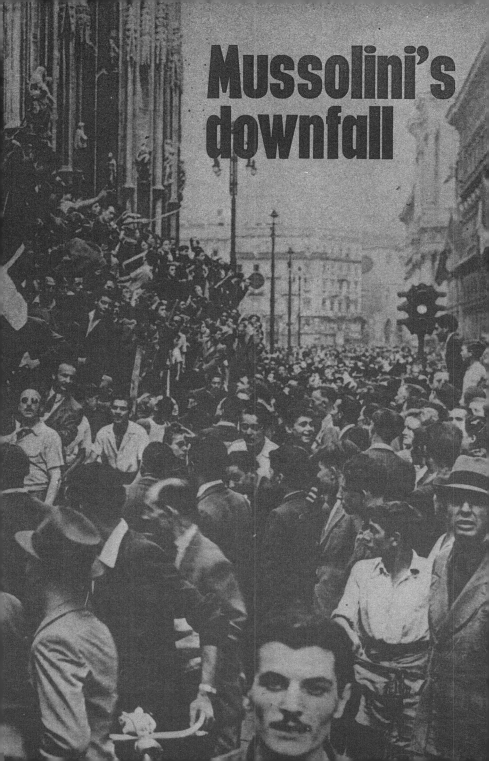

Mussolini's downfall

By this time, Mussolini's prestige had corroded to such an extent that at least three groups in Italy were plotting to overthrow him – dissident Fascists dissatisfied with the course of the war and uneasy over the failures and weakness of the regime, anti-Fascist politicians, and disenchanted military men. All were motivated by the need to remove the Duce from power as the essential first step of getting Italy out of the war, and the Allied bombing of Rome, serving notice on the imminent bankruptcy of Fascism, had been the last straw.

Apparently sensing his weakening influence in the country, Mussolini acted to gain a vote of confidence on the second day after he returned from his talk with Hitler. He summoned the Fascist Grand Council, which had not sat in session for more than three years, to a meeting on 24th July; but one day after he called the meeting, he visited Victor Emmanuel to inform him of his action. The King replied, but somewhat indirectly, that Mussolini ought to resign from office and a meeting of the Grand Council would be a suitable opportunity to make his resignation known. Mussolini professed not to understand.

Immediately after the Duce departed, Victor Emmanuel came to a long deferred decision. Having previously consulted with Maresciallo d'Italia Pietro Badoglio, war hero and former chief of Comando Supremo, who had assured the King that he would do whatever the monarch wished, Victor Emmanuel decided to appoint Badoglio as Mussolini's successor. Badoglio's task would be to break the alliance with Germany and make peace with the Allies.

Two days later, on 24th July, the Grand Council of 28 members met at 5 pm in formal session. A resolution was immediately introduced in favour of having the King supplant Mussolini as the supreme commander of the armed forces, and debate on this motion seemed interminable; it lasted for nine hours. Around 3 am, 25th July, Mussolini finally acceded to demands for a vote – and 19 members cast their ballots for the resolution: against Mussolini.

Later that day, Mussolini visited the King to advise him on what had taken place. He discussed the outcome of the vote and said that it did not require his resignation, but Victor Emmanuel differed with this interpretation. Coldly, he informed Mussolini that he would have to resign so that Badoglio could take his place.

When Mussolini left the palace, he was unable to find his car. Accepting the solicitude of a carabinieri officer, he was escorted to an ambulance, helped inside, and whisked away to a secret hiding place. He then discovered that he was under arrest.

News of Mussolini's dismissal raced through Rome and produced instantaneous joy. Strangers embraced and danced in the streets, citizens paraded spontaneously in gratitude to the King's palace. Mobs attacked Fascist party offices and tore down party flags and symbols.

At 5 pm in the midst of the celebrations, the King summoned Badoglio. Informing the aged field-marshal that he was now the head of government in place of Mussolini, Victor Emmanuel handed him a list of names of civil servants without party connection or support that Badoglio was to elevate to Cabinet rank, and armed with this royal mandate Badoglio announced his cabinet appointments, dissolved the Fascist party, and warned the Italian people against agitating for political change and immediate peace. 'The war continues,' he proclaimed. Although his policy, in compliance with the monarch's wishes, was to find a way to terminate Italy's participation in the war – a policy he did not make public – the first thing he had to do was to avoid open conflict with the Germans.

The news of Mussolini's overthrow enraged Hitler. His immediate reaction, born of wrath, was to fulminate against the treacherous Italians, threatening that he would seize Rome and take the King, the Crown Prince, Badoglio, and high-ranking officials prisoner. He would move a strong military force into northern Italy and treat it like occupied territory, find and liberate Mussolini and restore him to power, and then withdraw all the

A regime toppled. Mussolini's dismissal was greeted jubilantly by the Italian crowds ●

German troops at once from Sicily and southern Italy, even if their heavy equipment and weapons had to be left in place.

Jodl told him that it would be difficult to evacuate Sicily in a giant mass movement, for the ferrying facilities at Messina could accommodate only 17,000 men per day.

'Well,' Hitler exclaimed, 'they'll have to crowd together. Do you remember how it was at Dunkirk?'

Accordingly, Jodl sent Kesselring a message that night ordering him to move the German troops off the island – but before doing anything at all, Kesselring went to see Badoglio on 26th July. He listened to Badoglio's protestations that no change in policy was contemplated, to his reaffirmation that the Italians were determined to continue to fight alongside the Germans, and when Kesselring pointed out that it was necessary to overcome the sense of fatigue among the Italian troops and to eliminate certain impediments to the prosecution of the military effort raised by the civilian administration, Badoglio hastened to assure him that he would do everything he could to facilitate the conduct of the war.

Kesselring then called on Ambrosio, who repeated Badoglio's asseverations, emphasizing that the Italians were willing to continue in the war and to receive additional reinforcement.

Kesselring then sent a recommendation to Hitler. He suggested that the Germans exploit the willingness of the Italians to receive more German units. The more troops the Germans had in Italy, the easier it would be to insure their safety if Badoglio and the Italians defected.

Hitler thought this a clever idea. Having calmed down, he agreed that it would be best to make no precipitate move to break the alliance or to create turmoil that the Allies could take advantage of; better to pretend that all was well, to accept Italian declarations of continuing the alliance and the war, and to keep the Allied bombers as far from Germany as possible.

He ordered two divisions to be moved from southern France to the Italian border, there to be prepared to enter northern Italy in case of what he

Benito Mussolini in 1943

termed Italian treachery; he sent several officers to Rome with the secret mission of locating and rescuing Mussolini; he instructed Kesselring to to halt the movement of additiona[l] troops to Sicily; he directed him to prepare for the eventual evacuation of all the German units not only from Sicily but also from Sardinia and Corsica.

To prevent the leakage of plans to the Italians, Kesselring called a conference of senior German commanders on 27th July. He informed them that if the Italians left the alliance the XIV Panzer Corps was to disengage immediately and depart Sicily but until then, the Germans were to fight a delaying action and conserve their resources to the utmost. Meanwhile, they were to start drawing up detailed plans for abandoning the island. The movement of troops was to be co-ordinated by the XIV Panzer Corps headquarters in Sicily and the LXXVI Panzer Corps headquarters located in southern Italy; that evening, Hube instructed Baade to be sure he was ready for the mass evacuation whenever it was ordered into effect.

Ready with a detailed evacuation plan by August 2nd, Hube submitted it for approval to Kesselring. According to the estimates, all German troops and material could be transferred to the Italian mainland in five successive nights – so Kesselring approved the plan, telling Hube he would let him know when to start putting it into effect, and informing OKW that all was in readiness.

By then, a handful of Italian politi[cians]

King Victor Emmanuel

Marshal Pietro Badoglio

cal and military authorities under Badoglio's direction were setting out to make contact with the Allies for the purpose of arranging an armistice.

By then too, most Italians were expecting Badoglio to bring the war to an end. Italian resistance in Sicily had virtually collapsed, many troops simply going through the motions of obeying orders and seeking instead to be taken prisoner. According to an Allied intelligence summary, published on 27th July 'Sheer war weariness and a feeling of the hopelessness of Italy's position have . . . permeated the field army to a considerable degree, with the result that a sense of inferiority and futility has destroyed its zest and spirit.'

Not so the Germans, who sought to inflict as much damage on the Allied forces as they could in the difficult terrain of northeastern Sicily, even as they pulled back slowly. Only two real questions remained to be answered: when would Hitler order the movement to the mainland to start, and could the Germans prevent the Allies from pushing them off the island in rout?

On 26th July, the day after Mussolini's dismissal and arrest, the Combined Chiefs of Staff met in Washington while Eisenhower's principal subordinates met with him in Algiers, to consider whether, and how best, to exploit this sudden change in the situation. The outlook in both cities was optimistic. A descent on the mainland near Naples now seemed altogether feasible, and it would strengthen the new Italian government and embarrass the Germans – but

unfortunately no immediate move could be made, primarily because most of the landing craft that had participated in the invasion of Sicily were being repaired and refitted. Mainly for this reason the Allied leaders decided to hold off making a final selection of the next target area until after the Sicily campaign was over.

Yet all were agreed that a landing near Naples, now crystallizing into an invasion along the Salerno beaches, looked good, and there was also a resurgence of talk in favour of an ad hoc invasion across the Strait of Messina to complement the main venture at Salerno. On 2nd August after much thought and discussion, Eisenhower finally decided; he would launch a twin invasion of the mainland, rushing part of Montgomery's Eighth Army across the strait upon completion of the Sicily campaign and at the same time going for the big operation at Salerno.

The Combined Chiefs were agreeable.

A week later, on 10th August, Eisenhower halted planning for an impromptu invasion across the Strait of Messina, stressing that he wanted well-prepared operations, there as well as at Salerno. But still no final decision was propounded; this would await the conquest of all Sicily.

As for the campaign in Sicily, the elimination of Mussolini had no significant impact on the Allied troops or on the conduct of operations. The end of the war seemed suddenly much closer, but there was no change in the method being followed to conquer Sicily.

The Etna line

As early as 22nd July Allied intelligence officers were accurately describing Hube's Etna Line. Where they were wrong was their guess that the Germans would fall back to other more highly organized final positions they were building behind the Etna defences. The final defences, the Allied commanders believed, would serve the Germans as a springboard for a vigorous counterattack or as a screen for withdrawal to the mainland.

Actually, Hube had no concept of a final defensive line. The northwestern corner of Sicily gave him excellent ground for establishing any number of strongpoints, where small garrisons could be highly effective, holding hilltop towns or mountain passes, and thus blocking Allied frontal advances and forcing the attackers into tortuous outflanking movements across rugged, virtually impassible terrain. When outflanked or threatened with encirclement, the small delaying group could simply pull out, usually during the night, to another blocking position previously prepared.

This was what Bradley's II Corps came up against when the two divisions started their drive along the two roads in the northern part of the island – Highway 113 along the coast, and Highway 120 through Nicosia, Troina, Cesaro, and Randazzo. Both highways were narrow and crooked, with steep grades and sharp turns, bridges and tunnels that could easily be destroyed by demolition. Between the roads and parallel to them ran the Caronie Mountain chain, with very few lateral roads across the range. The troops had the sensation of moving over a washboard, creased by streams flowing at frequent intervals from the mountain tops to the sea.

Moreover, the 45th Division along the coastal road and the 1st Division on the inland route were separated and unable to be mutually supporting, so each division had to fight its own war, which for both soon became a matter of short flanking marches over very rugged hills, a process terribly hard on the troops. But the alternative was worse – as Allen said, 'Had we kept up just a frontal attack, it would have meant just a bloody nose for us at every hill.'

Middleton's 45th Division, turning eastward from Termini Imerese, came abreast of the 1st Division on 24th July, despite demolished bridges and mine fields created as obstacles by German troops. Since Hube was erecting his defences in that sector, the 45th Division made excellent progress which came to a sudden halt on 25th July when 14 unidentified warships appeared off the northern shore. Concerned that they were Axis ships bringing troops to an amphibious landing, Bradley stopped Middleton's advance and faced the division out to sea.

Hube saw the same vessels, and he feared they were moving Allied amphibious forces to a landing behind his line. He alerted Axis units all the way back to Calabria to be ready to repel a landing – but the vessels turned out to be American destroyers and mine sweepers on a routine mission unrelated to the ground warfare.

The threat of amphibious landings altogether imaginary in this case gave additional urgency to Hube's desire to consolidate his defences When his chief of staff returned to Sicily – he had attended the meeting that Kesselring had called near Rome on 27th July to discuss Hitler's reaction to Mussolini's dismissal, and the German course of action following Mussolini's downfall – Hube pulled back his troops from Nicosia.

Guzzoni protested, for Nicosia was a highly defensible point. When Hube explained that his primary mission had become the need to secure the forces on the island and prepare them for evacuation, Guzzoni conceded that the Axis could not long hold the island with the troops then committed. The reinforced Hermann Göring Division in the Catania area appeared capable of blocking the British advance to Messina, but the 15th and 29th Panzer Grenadier Divisions, despite augmentation by the 1st Parachute Division and what remained of the Italian divisions, were having difficulty holding against the pressure of the Americans and Canadians in the northern and central sectors. He accepted the necessity to pull back to a shorter

The defenders. *Above:* wounded being evacuated. *Below:* the command post of an artillery position

ront.

The German withdrawal during the night of 27th July gave Nicosia to the Americans, who captured 700 Italian soldiers eager to surrender, and Agira to the Canadians.

To American intelligence officers who were looking for the German final defence line, the withdrawal from Nicosia and Agira seemed to indicate that the Germans were getting ready for a final stand. 'The successful defense of Catania and the Catania Plain have (sic) raised German morale and hopes to the point where they are willing to gamble two or three more divisions to hold a Sicilian bridgehead,' read a report dated 28th July. Indications,' read another two days later, 'are that the enemy is falling back to that area.'

The belief was prevalent that Hitler was going to try to hang on to a permanent bridgehead in Sicily - like the Salonika bridgehead held by the Allied Powers in World War I or the bridgehead that Hitler had hoped to keep in Tunisia. In the view of American intelligence officers, therefore, everything forward of the imaginary final defence line was to be given up.

This seemed to be the case with Troina. 'Germans very tired,' the 1st Division intelligence officer reported on 29th July, 'little ammo, many casualties, morale low.' Two days later: 'Indications are Troina lightly held.'

Reconnaissance pilots could find very little evidence of strong defences around Troina. They reported only light traffic through the town - which seemed to be another place manned by a skeleton garrison that would fight a brief delaying action before pulling out.

Thus, on the last day of July, an infantry regiment of the 1st Division jumped off at dawn from Nicosia toward Cerami with the expectation of continuing through Cerami to Troina, seven miles away. By nine o'clock, troops were in Cerami with hardly any trouble at all and optimism soared. Civilians said that the garrison in

Troina had few troops, only a few anti-tank guns, and a single anti-aircraft battery, and since everyone expected Troina to fall easily, Allen, who was to turn over his division front to the 9th Division after he captured Troina, felt what he later called a moral obligation to give the incoming division 'a tight sector.'

Beyond Cerami, the single committed regiment ran into difficulties, and Allen found himself gradually committing increasing forces to the battle. 'I think there is a hell of a lot of stuff there up near our objective,' a regimental commander reported on 1st August. Another remarked 'a very strong defence' and questioned whether 'we have strength enough to do the job.' Still another telephoned to division headquarters that his men were 'Moving right into the teeth of the enemy.'

Before Troina fell, five American regiments - all three of the 1st Division and two of the 9th - would be committed against the defenders of Troina.

The point was that Troina, a town of 12,000 people built on a high and dominating bluff, was a natural defensive position. In addition, Troina had great significance for the integrity of the entire Etna Line, for loss of the town would threaten the key points of Regalbuto, Adrano, and Catania.

For that reason, Hube watched Troina carefully.

He also gave close attention to the sector immediately to the south, where Canadian troops were advancing along Highway 121. Early on 30th July the Canadians struck hard and cleared Catenanuova, and Major-General G. G. Simonds, commander of the 1st Canadian Division, then gave part of his bridgehead to the newly arrived 78th Division, thus making possible an attack toward Regalbuto on the left and Centuripe on the right. Regalbuto fell to the Canadians on the evening of the 2nd August; Centuripe, built on a high mountain reached by a single, twisting road, was stormed by the 78th Division on the morning of 3rd August.

This put the two main outposts of Adrano in British hands, and Adrano, like Troina, was a key position in the Etna Line. If the Canadian and British divisions pressed farther, the escape

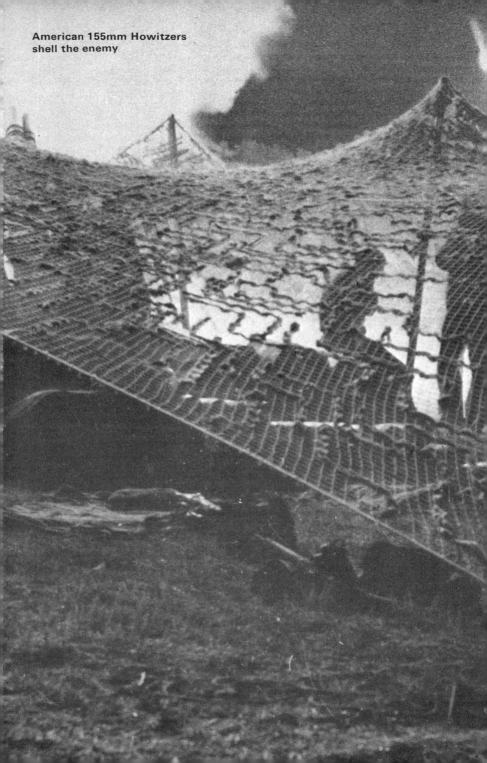
American 155mm Howitzers
shell the enemy

Italian packhorses. The mountainous terrain made communications difficult,

route of the bulk of Rodt's 15th Panzer Grenadier Division defending Troina might be cut – and by the end of 3rd August, these had taken heavy losses of at least 1,600 casualties. That night Hube gave Rodt the last of his corps reserves to enable him to hold open an escape route east of the town, but since Kesselring had not yet formally ordered the evacuation of Sicily to begin, Hube decided to hold the Etna Line as long as he could. He told Rodt to stand fast.

On the morning of 4th August two large-scale Allied air attacks struck Troina. Reactions from the American ground troops struggling toward the town were uniformly enthusiastic. 'Air and arty bombardment lovely,' one unit reported. 'The enemy is com-

pletely unnerved,' reported another. 'Have captured a few Germans and they are jittery,' said a third.

But the gains on the ground were slight.

In fact, the Canadian reaction to the air attack was a furious protest, for two planes had dropped their bombs on Canadian troops in Regalbuto by mistake, and Leese asked Bradley to keep American planes away from the British front.

By this time, the 9th Division under Major-General Manton S. Eddy, was moving into Nicosia behind the 1st Division. To let the 9th pass through and smash the next German defensive line (which was expected to be uncovered in the Cesaro area), the 1st Division had first to take Troina, and no one was optimistic any longer about a quick triumph.

Montgomery, meanwhile, had chan-

ged to some extent the thrust of his attacks. Because the decision seemed certain that British troops would cross the Strait of Messina and invade the toe of Italy at the end of the Sicily campaign, Montgomery began to devote his attention to the best way of regrouping his forces to facilitate the crossing. He decided to send Dempsey's XIII Corps across the strait, which meant that Leese's XXX Corps would finish the fighting in Sicily, and as soon as the two thrusts around Mount Etna met, he planned to rest the 1st Canadian and 5th Divisions of the XIII Corps and prepare for the assault on the Italian mainland. The XXX Corps, with the 50th, 51st, and 78th Divisions, would complete the Sicily campaign.

Thus, he ordered Leese to make his main effort toward Adrano, while Dempsey stood on the alert along the eastern coast ready to seize Catania when the opportunity arose.

The opportunity appeared on 3rd August after Hube told Conrath to start thinning his defences in front of Catania preparatory to withdrawing. Noticing the movements, Dempsey sent the British 5th Division into attack that night, but strong rearguards of the Hermann Göring Division contested the British advance; not until the afternoon of 4th August had the 5th Division moved forward four miles to the southern outskirts of Catania. After an all-night battle and following the retirement of Conrath's rearguards, British troops moved to the edge of the city.

The drive to Adrano had continued, but slowly because of a plethora of mines and demolitions left by the Germans to delay progress. It was difficult to deploy troop units off the

Left: 500 pound bombs being dropped on Catania from a height of 20,000 feet.
Above: South African Bren gun carriers pass through Centuripe

indifferent roads running through extensive lava belts and terraced farms, but as British and Canadians pushed relentlessly, Adrano finally fell. With that, the Etna Line was broken.

Although Rodt still held the vital heights of Troina at the end of 5th August, it was obvious that he could not hold much longer. His units depleted, his men near exhaustion, Rodt asked Hube's permission to withdraw three miles to a new defensive line. Hube at first refused, later relented. The reduced combat efficiency of Rodt's division, the lack of German reserves, the danger of an Allied breakthrough in the Troina-Cesaro sector, and the possibility of amphibious landings in his rear prompted Hube to give Rodt permission to withdraw to what Guzzoni called the Tortorici line – a series of defensive positions from Cape Orlando on the northern coast, through Poggio del Moro, Randazzo, Mount Etna, to Giarre on the eastern shore.

That night of 5th August, while Rodt pulled his forces back from Troina, Conrath, in compliance with Hube's instructions, withdrew his Hermann Göring Division from Catania.

British troops thus entered Catania after nearly a month of endeavour, and American troops moved into the ruins of Troina after six days of attack. Both towns were smashed by bombs and shells, and the dust of broken plaster carried the stench of death. In Troina the Americans found 150 civilians and soldiers, German and Italian, lying dead in the streets; rubble blocked the roads, the main street was blown away, and a 200-pound aerial bomb lay unexploded in the centre of the church.

In the meantime, the Hermann Göring Division occupied new defensive positions north of Catania, and the 15th Panzer Grenadier Division dug in along a new fortified line near Cesaro, though much of the heavy equipment of both divisions was on its way to Messina for eventual shipment across the strait.

The same sort of events, but with a different twist, took place on the coastal road in the north where Truscott's 3rd Division, having re-

Above: Mopping up in a small town.
Below: Catania falls to the British.
Below right: Victims of the Allied advance

placed the 45th, could make its main effort along the highway or across the northern slopes of the Caronie Mountains to outflank the German defenders. Either way the Germans had the advantage. They could deny the use of the highway by fire, demolitions, and mines, and they could delay inland by defensive positions along well defined ridgelines behind deeply cut mountain streams. But the Americans held a trump card – the means of making amphibious end-runs around the German defences.

By the beginning of August, fully appreciating that the tangled mountains of northeastern Sicily would deny him the slashing armoured drives he had unleashed in the west toward Palermo, Patton looked to the technique of seaborne landing to move his troops forward. Messina, the strategic culmination, the tactical climax of the campaign, lay ahead, and the more he thought of getting to Messina, the more he became excited by and obsessed with the idea of getting there ahead of Montgomery.

On 2nd August, Patton decided he would definitely employ amphibious landings to hasten his progress to Messina. There were plenty of good beaches for landing sites, and the only trouble was that the available landing craft could lift only one reinforced infantry battalion, no more – and this was hardly a formidable force to get behind the German forces which, in retreat, would let nothing stand in their way of escape.

But since no additional boats could be obtained, Patton would make do with what he had. His staff selected four tentative landing sites, each behind a predictable defensive line, where a battalion might come ashore to pry loose the coastal anchor of defensive positions. These were near Sant'Agata, Brolo, Patti, and Barcellona; but Bradley, fearing that Patton in his intense desire to get to Messina quickly might be rash in ordering a seaborne landing, secured his agreement that amphibious operations would be closely co-ordinated with the overland advances of the major part of the division to insure swift link-up of both forces. Otherwise, the amphibious force might be isolated and destroyed.

The 3rd Division jumped off on the morning of 4th August and was stopped cold. There were 103 casualties, and no ground was taken, for the division had bumped into the San Fratello line, held by the 29th Panzer Grenadier Division, commanded by Major-General Walter Fries. Harassed by American artillery and naval gunfire and by air strikes, Fries had built a strong line of defence replete with pillboxes, trenches, and gun emplacements difficult to eradicate in the excellent defensive terrain; and when Truscott's troops jumped off again on the morning of 5th August, the Germans again refused to be dislodged.

In part, Fries held his positions because they were superb; in part, he was insuring, by his tenacity, an orderly withdrawal from the San Fratello ridge whenever he got word to pull back. When he learned that Rodt was about to give up Troina, which would uncover his left flank, and when he understood that the 78th Division was nearing Adrano and the Hermann Göring Division was giving up Catania, he started to send detachments to the rear, meanwhile holding fast to the San Fratello heights.

On 6th August seeing no result to the incessant pounding of his artillery bolstered by naval gunfire, Truscott decided that outflanking the San Fratello line by sea was the least costly way to eliminate the defensive positions. He ordered the operation to go ahead that night.

Late that afternoon, as the battalion designated to make the amphibious landing was marching to its embarkation point near Santo Stefano, four German aircraft bombed and strafed the area. Two planes were shot down by anti-aircraft fire, but a key vessel in the projected amphibious assault, an LTS, was damaged beyond repair, so Truscott postponed the operation for another 24 hours, and the naval authorities rushed another LST from Palermo.

During 7th August pressure by the 3rd Division cracked the San Fratello positions, and Fries was ready to pull back during the night. That afternoon, the battalion selected for the amphibious end run was again marching to the Santo Stefano beaches when

Eighth Army men storm a station
Right: Italian prisoners usually looked
happy

another German air raid materialized,
bombs damaged the newly arrived
LST and an escort vessel, but hurried
repairs made the LST seaworthy
enough to sail. In the evening, covered
by two cruisers and six destroyers, the
ten landing craft of the assault pulled
away from the Santo Stefano beaches.
At the same time, although American
warships were shelling the San Fratello ridge almost constantly, Fries
pulled out the rest of his division,
leaving the Assietta Division on the
ridge to cover his withdrawal.

Thus when the American infantry
battalion came ashore just east of
Sant'Agata at 3.15 in the morning of
8th August, the Germans were gone,
and when the 3rd Division attacked the
San Fratello ridge at dawn, the troops
met very little opposition from the
Assietta Division. Feeling abandoned
by the Germans, exhausted by the
fighting and the heat, Italian soldiers
surrendered in droves.

Fries's division meanwhile moved
into another set of fortified positions.

The evacuation

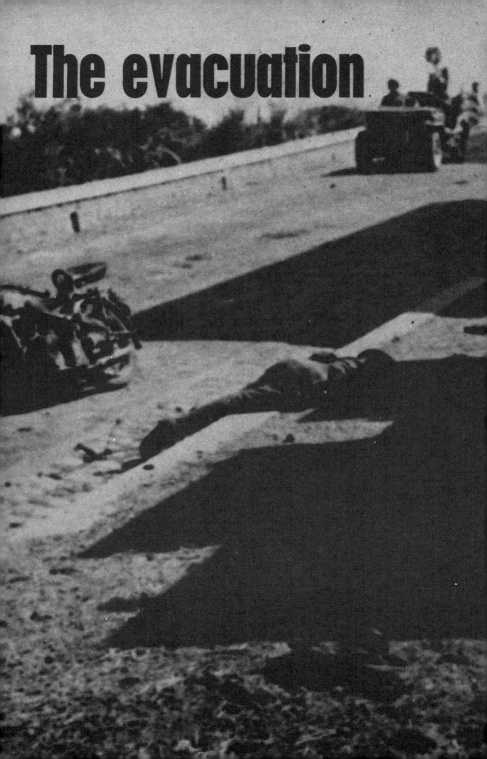

The Italo-German alliance was nothing more than a pretence by the beginning of August. While Comando Supremo continued a wary co-operation with the Germans, Italian emissaries from the Badoglio government were secretly meeting with Allied representatives in Lisbon and Tangier to arrange surrender. The Germans practised a forced cordiality toward the Italians that was transparently false, meanwhile watching everywhere for defection or capitulation. Having moved and stationed sufficient German forces around Rome to insure its capture should that drastic action become necessary, OKW on 5th August was content to remain on the alert. Headquarters – mainly because the Germans were still unable to locate Mussolini as the ever-helpful Italian counter-espionage service was providing a variety of false leads – cancelled plans that had earlier been drawn for the seizure of Rome and the capture of the members of the Italian government.

Kesselring had helped convince OKW to postpone the actual seizure of Rome because he felt that the Italians would turn on the Germans, who would then be forced to withdraw all their units from Sicily and southern Italy. Believing that the Italians were genuinely willing to co-operate, he hoped to hold on to Sicily as long as he could in order to tie down the dozen or so Allied divisions engaged there.

Jodl felt, on the contrary, that the Allies in Sicily were tying down German divisions. If the Allies landed in southern Italy before the Germans got out of Sicily, they would bag the entire XIV Panzer Corps on the island; and they would be able to advance against little opposition to the northern Apennines, for the few units in southern Italy were too weak to impede a full-scale Allied offensive. He advocated an immediate withdrawal from Sicily and southern Italy.

Hitler could not make up his mind. He was determined to send no more reinforcements to Sicily or to southern Italy, but he could not decide to withdraw. He wanted to find Mussolini first. Until the special investigators sent to Rome succeeded in liberating Mussolini, Hitler instructed Kesselring to observe the appearance of good faith in the Badogli government.

Among Badoglio's earliest acts wa a request for a personal meeting wit Hitler. Since Badoglio had proclaime that the Italians would continue th war beside the Germans, howeve Hitler saw no reason for a conferenc though he acceded to a meeting of th German and Italian foreign ministe and chiefs of staff.

This conference took place at Tr viso, just across the Italian border, o 6th August. Solemn and meaningle statements were expressed by parti pants on both sides, exploring ho best to continue the war rather tha how best to make peace. Both we stalling for time – the Italians awai ing an Allied response to their ove tures for capitulation, the Germa awaiting the rescue of Mussolini. T only result of the meeting was a intensification of mutual suspicion.

Hitler became convinced that t Italians would soon defect; in h words, they were planning treaso and he ordered a wide variety of plan and actions prepared to cope with wide variety of alternatives. Whe would the Italians capitulate? Wou the Allies invade southern Italy Would they do so after a promise Italian assistance?

Although Kesselring made grea efforts to prevent a harsh and susp cious attitude on the part of Germar from completely alienating th Italians, OKW went ahead with plan to seize the Italian fleet, to tak Rome, and to convert the Italia peninsula into a battlefield for th defence of Germany. So many Germa troops had entered northern Italy b then, the region appeared occupied.

For their part, the Italians on 10t August sent a secret order to all the principal military forces and installa tions; commanders were forewarne that they were to resist any surpris German attack or any German vic lence against military facilities.

Meanwhile, Hube had urged Guzzo on 5th August to transfer his Sixt Army headquarters to the mainlan for Hube wanted a completely fre hand in arranging the final defenc

American infantrymen advance gingerly along a cliff

and the ultimate evacuation of troops from the island. However, although the Italians had already started a limited withdrawal from Sicily two days earlier, Guzzoni refused to go completely; he remained to safeguard Italian interests.

Exactly when the Germans would give up Sicily had yet to be determined, and the matter of timing concerned Kesselring. Since Hitler was always reluctant to give up ground, Kesselring feared that the Führer would be too dilatory in deciding to abandon Sicily, and in view of the disastrous consequences that had resulted from Hitler's unwillingness to leave Tunisia in time, Kesselring decided to issue the evacuation order himself.

By 8th August it seemed that the time had come for that decision. Fries had pulled back from San Fratello, just in time it appeared, to avoid being cut off by amphibious landing; Rodt had withdrawn from Cesaro; the town of Bronte had fallen that morning to the 78th Division, and the British XIII Corps was eight miles beyond Catania and exerting heavy pressure on Conrath's division. On that day, von Senger flew to Kesselring's headquarters and reported that the situation in Sicily was serious if not precisely critical. All the forces were still holding fast, but they would be unable to do so for much longer.

Without informing Hitler or requesting permission from OKW, Kesselring ordered Hube to go ahead with the evacuation of the island.

OKW learned of Kesselring's order on the following day, and Jodl, 'in his calm way', as Jodl's deputy recalled after the war, 'succeeded in guiding Hitler to undesirable but necessary decisions' – meaning approval.

When Guzzoni learned of Kesselring's order on 9th August, he examined the possibility of continuing the defence of Sicily with Italian forces alone, but soon concluded that this would be senseless. The Italian troops might delay the Allied occupation of the entire island for a few days, but the price in terms of human sacrifice was out of proportion to the potential advantages to be gained.

He simply informed Comando Supremo of the German decision, a which that body instructed Guzzoni t leave the island and take over th defence of Calabria. He was to accele rate the evacuation of Italian force and start the rearward movement i earnest.

Late in the afternoon of 10th Augus as Guzzoni and his Sixth Army head quarters were crossing the Strait Messina, Hube issued his formal ord for evacuation. The withdrawal fro Sicily would start during the night 11th August and continue for fo more nights.

Whether the Germans would succee in leaving Sicily would depend on th discipline of commanders at a echelons, on their ability to follo meticulous schedules without pani and ultimately on their confidenc that everyone else was gearing h activities to the methodical arrang ments prepared for the withdrawal.

Yet in the final analysis, the respo sibility for success or failure woul devolve in large measure on one ma Baade, who exercised control ov both sides of the Messina strait. Und him were all the German enginee artillery, anti-aircraft and naval uni in the area – in short, all the tran portation and security units require for a mass movement involving tho sands of troops and their equipmen

To defend the strait against Alli air and naval attack, Baade had abo 500 guns, most of them equipped fire against ground targets as well aircraft. What Allied officers ha characterized in 1942 and early 19 as one of the most heavily defende areas in Europe had become by Augu probably the best protected. Accor ing to an experienced Allied air sta officer, the anti-aircraft fire was 'th heaviest ever encountered in th Mediterranean – heavier than 'Fla Alley' between Bizerta and Tunis, a greater than the inner artillery London'.

Under this formidable barrier fire, Baade had three naval flotilla an engineer landing battalion, two three engineer fortification batt lions, and two port maintenance con panies. They all worked to opera 33 naval barges similar to Alli LCTs, 12 Siebel ferries – 10-ton fla bottomed multi-purpose supply a

The Flakvierling 20mm Model 38. This German light anti-aircraft gun is shown here in its emplaced role. Its high rate of fire and wide traverse made it ideal against fast low level aircraft. *Weight:* 3,330 pounds. *Traverse:* 360 degrees. *Crew:* 5 or 6. *Rate of fire:* 800 rounds per minute. *Range:* 4,800 yards. *Muzzle velocity:* 2,800 feet per second

Boeing B-17F
Engines: Four Wright R-1820-97, 1,200 hp *Armament:* Ten or eleven .50-inch machine guns and up to 8,000 lbs of bombs *Maximum speed:* 299 mph at 25,000 feet *Ceiling:* 37,500 feet *Range:* 1,300 miles with 6,000 lbs bombload 3,880 milex max *Weight empty:* 34,000 lbs *Weight loaded:* 55,000 lbs-56,500 lbs *Span:* 103 feet 9 inches *Length:* 74 feet 9 inches

The camouflage netting of a 105mm gun catches fire

troop carriers, two naval gun lighters, 11 barges used as engineer landing craft, and 76 motor-boats.

Baade developed six ferry routes, with each having several landing places on either shore. Hube selected four routes as being the most practical – they were all north of Messina – and a fifth route south of Messina to be used only in emergency.

Hube designated the two northern-most routes at the tip of Sicily to be reserved for the 15th and 29th Panzer Grenadier Divisions, in that order, a third route, two miles north of Messina, to be used for the XIV Panzer Corps headquarters, miscellaneous troops, and overflow. The fourth, one mile north of Messina, was for the Hermann Göring Division and the attached elements of the 1st Parachute Division. Other German units were to cross on any route on a space-available basis.

He specified that troops were to cross only during the hours of darkness. Weapons and equipment were to be ferried over day and night accord-

ing to a strict priority established anti-tank weapons, artillery piec self-propelled weapons, trucks, a motor vehicles, in that order, and material unable to be taken off island was to be destroyed. Lieutena General Richard Heidrich, comm der of the 1st Parachute Divisi was to organize reception facilities Calabria. The boats available co transport about 8,000 men each nig and in order to insure a smooth mo ment without bottlenecks and c gestion, the right number of men l to be at proper embarkation points the right time.

Hube planned to hold the Torto line until 12th August. Then he wo move his forces back in three stag delaying at successive phase li across the northeastern tip of island until everyone was out. 15th Panzer Grenadier Division wa start moving through Randazzo 10th August to the two ferry routes the end of the island and be off 15th August. The 29th Panzer Gr adier Division was to follow, and

the same time, the Hermann Göring Division was to pull back around both sides of Mount Etna. The whole movement was to be regulated by a meticulous schedule of phase lines and checkpoints to insure a steady stream of men and material across the strait.

In similar fashion, the Italians organized four ferry routes – two from the port of Messina and two from points north of the city. They had one train ferry capable of lifting 3,000 men per trip, two small steamboats, and four motor-boats. They were unable to transport heavy equipment, but Hube generously offered to take whatever he could according to whatever space might be available on German craft.

The Allies were quite aware of the Axis intention to evacuate Sicily. As early as 3rd August, Alexander believed that the Germans would start back almost any time, and he requested Cunningham and Tedder to co-ordinate naval and air efforts to disrupt the ferries. Two days later, the Seventh Army G-2, taking note of the limited Italian movements, announced that 'in all probability

evacuation is taking place'. On 9th August British intelligence reported somewhat prematurely, 'From now on it seems to be a question of who can walk back the fastest. The Germans are definitely getting out everything they can.'

Despite their realization of the Axis withdrawal policy, the Allied leaders came up with no overall plan to thwart it. In reply to Alexander's request for co-ordinated air and naval action, Cunningham said that he had small craft operating at night in the straits to counter the movement of Axis troops and material, but he could not, he added, employ larger warships until the air forces knocked out the strong coastal batteries. Meanwhile, he promised that the activities of the small boats would be 'intensified' and that once the batteries were eliminated by air bombardment, he would send substantial 'surface forces to operate further in the straits.'

Tedder put the air forces to work immediately, but it was less than a massive effort. Crews were weary, the anti-aircraft defences were fearsome, and air units were already attacking airfields, railroads, and bridges in the Italian mainland as a preliminary for an invasion of southern Italy. Between 5th and 9th August British medium Wellington bombers struck the beaches north of Messina every night, and American B-17s flew three daylight missions against Messina itself, but the results of these operations convinced air commanders that unless warships could provide a 'positive physical barrier' at night across the strait, air attack could not prevent the evacuation.

Cunningham gave 'the matter very careful thought' once more. And in the end, he felt that there was no 'effective method' of stopping the evacuation by 'sea or air'. The only positive way of interfering with, disrupting, or preventing the movement of Axis forces across the strait was by ground action – the ground forces had to reach the evacuation beaches before all the Axis forces could depart.

On 8th August when Kesselring gave Hube the green light for evacuating Sicily, Montgomery's Eighth Army was 52 miles from Messina, Patton's Seventh Army 75 miles. Facing them were forces obstinately fighting to preserve their escape routes in rugged terrain that offered few natural channels of advance to Messina, and the diminishing length of the front as they moved into the narrowing corner of Sicily permitted enemy troops to be pulled out without weakening the successively shorter defensive lines. To break up the mass withdrawal, the Allied ground forces must get to Messina before the Axis troops were ready to leave, and since frontal assault on the tenacious defenders was costly and promised no swift progress, the Allied commanders looked to two other methods of advance – amphibious landings or airborne drops behind the enemy front to cut the last few remaining withdrawal routes.

Montgomery had actually embarked a large Commando force twice in landing craft to speed up the east coast and trap the withdrawing Germans, but he had cancelled both operations because he considered them too risky. He had also executed four small airborne operations designed to harass the enemy with-

drawal, three consisting of airborne jumps from two planes, one an airborne drop from a single plane; but they were far too small to interfere substantially with the German and Italian movements.

Apparently already preoccupied with the forthcoming invasion of Calabria that was to take place once the Sicily campaign was completed, Montgomery preferred to push forward slowly and meticulously around Mount Etna, using much the same plan he had developed four days after the invasion.

Patton kept the battalion task force that had made the end-run to Sant'-Agata intact and planned to use it again whenever a favourable opportunity arose, and he also prepared to use a parachute battalion to drop astride the German withdrawal routes – but by this time, the desire to beat Montgomery to Messina was infecting not only Patton but most Americans. The British Broadcasting Corporation, the principal radio station heard by the American troops in Sicily, had allegedly made an unfortunate comparison between the

operations of the two Allied armies, saying that the British Eighth Army was fighting hard while the American Seventh Army was having so easy a time that the troops were eating grapes and swimming in the warm sea. Infuriated by these disparaging comments (or at least by rumours of the remarks) the Americans, who still resented the subordinate mission earlier assigned them by Alexander, became doubly eager to reach Messina first.

On 9th August Patton ordered another amphibious end-run, this one to take place that night, but unfortunately, a Luftwaffe raid sank one of the LSTs earmarked to transport the battalion task force. On the following day, after another LST had been brought from Palermo, Patton summoned Bradley to his command post and instructed him to set the end-run in motion that evening.

The amphibious troops were to come ashore at Brolo, ten miles ahead of the 3rd Division's leading forces and informed by Bradley of Patton's wish, Truscott agreed. But later, when he learned that his division had not

Left: Sicilians watch from a rudimentary shelter. Above: A blood transfusion

made the progress expected that day, he wanted to postpone the operation for another 24 hours, a delay which would enable his troops to get closer to the landing site and make quick link-up feasible. Since the coastal route was obviously the main escape route for the 29th Panzer Grenadier Division, the Germans were likely to roll over and annihilate the small battalion task force of little more than 1,000 men.

While Truscott was debating the issue with his staff, Patton's deputy army commander, Keyes, arrived at the command post to see how the planning for the amphibious operation was coming along. Truscott said he wanted to postpone the landing, but Keyes doubted strongly that Patton would agreed to a postponement, for he had arranged for newspaper correspondents to accompany the landing force, and he would hate to tell the journalists that the end-run, already deferred once because an LST

had been sunk, was again being put off.

Truscott then telephoned II Corps, and explained the situation to Bradley who, agreeing that Truscott's caution was warranted, said he would phone Patton and try to secure his agreement for a postponement. When he called Truscott back, Bradley said that Patton insisted that the operation go forward, at which point Keyes telephoned Patton from Truscott's headquarters to add his urging for a delay.

Patton told Keyes to put Truscott on the phone. When Truscott complied Patton said shortly, 'Damn it, the operation will go on'.

There was no alternative but to transmit the order to the battalion task force, and as he did so, Truscott instructed every combat unit in the division to be committed in the attack on the following morning, to break through the German defences and link up quickly with the amphibious task force.

The division faced the Naso ridge, where Fries had his 29th Panzer Grenadier Division well dug in. Ten miles to the rear, near Brolo where the American battalion was to come ashore, Fries had stationed a fairly strong force, close to a regiment in strength, to guard against just the kind of landing that had been made at Sant'Agata. The German headquarters near Brolo was established on Monte Cipolla, a nose of the Caronie Mountains, several hundred yards inland and rising abruptly from a small coastal plain. This rise dominates the plain, the coastal highway, and the beach, and was in fact the objective of the battalion task force.

The American task force was loaded into an LST, two LCIs, and six LCTs by 6 pm on 10th August and the flotilla put to sea under the protection of the battleship *Philadelphia* and six destroyers. Arriving 3,000 yards off the shore near Brolo at 1 am on 11th August, the men clambered into LCVPs and DUKWs for the run to the beach; the boats of the first wave grounded on the sand about 2.30 am and the men splashed ashore. There was no opposition.

A B-17 delivers its load

The initial troops cut passages through a barbed wire fence, crossed the road and the railroad, captured ten Germans in a lemon grove without firing a shot, and set up blocks at the railroad and highway bridges crossing the Brolo River. By 4 am the other waves, including several tanks and four artillery pieces, were ashore, though the tanks and guns had some difficulty manoeuvering across the railroad embankment. Then the bulk of the force started moving up the slope of Monte Cipolla.

The Americans were still undetected when a German motorcycle dispatch rider roared down the highway. The men froze in place and allowed him to pass, but soon afterwards, a German halftrack approached, the driver noticed troops along the road, and halted his vehicle. As he rose from his seat to see who they were, about 20 anxious Americans opened fire and killed him; seconds later, a German military sedan came by and stopped. An officer stepped out to investigate the source of the gunfire, an American fired a bazooka that struck the sedan squarely, killed the officer, and wounded the driver.

This noise awakened all the Germans in the neighbourhood. Before long, fire was coming at the American troops from all directions, but they continued to move on Monte Cipolla, where the German headquarters consisted of 15 men, obviously too few to contest the hill. They scurried off the height by way of the rear slope, and the commander walked the short distance to Brolo and telephoned Fries. With his major escape route threatened, Fries moved to dispose of the small American force.

Except for the tanks and artillery pieces that were unable to negotiate the slope, most of the Americans were on top of Monte Cipolla and dug in by 5.30 am. They were none too soon, for German guns began to pound them, and although the battleship *Philadelphia* shelled prearranged targets and this was helpful, at 10.30 am, having completed the planned fire missions and having lost radio contact with the battalion ashore, the warship sailed off toward Palermo in order to avoid presenting a tempting target to the Luftwaffe.

Truscott, whose main attack with all units committed against the Naso ridge was progressing slowly, received word from the battalion on Monte Cipolla in midmorning. A high-powered radio set informed him that Fries had organized an attack designed to roll over the defenders on the hill, but Truscott's urgent messages to the naval authorities asking that warships return to Brolo were answered, and at 2 pm a cruiser and two destroyers were back at Brolo, firing against German positions. Truscott had also called Bradley about getting air strikes to support the besieged battalion, so in midafternoon 12 planes appeared and dropped bombs on Brolo, followed shortly by a dozen more. By this time, too, Truscott had also had his medium artillery pieces moved forward enough so that the shells, fired at maximum range, could reach Brolo.

Thus ringed by fire, the battalion held out, although its situation worsened as increasing numbers of German troops came into the area to contain at least, to eliminate if possible, this small force which threatened their withdrawal route.

Then at 4 pm seven Allied aircraft swept over Brolo, strafing and bombing the area; two bombs fell on the Americans, killing and wounding 19 men and knocking out all four of the artillery pieces. The battalion commander then consolidated his troops in a tight perimeter on Monte Cipolla and made ready for a last-ditch stand.

Soon afterwards, the *Philadelphia* returned on station off Brolo and plastered the countryside, but just before 5 pm eight German aircraft attacked the American warships, causing little damage to the ships which shot down several planes, but threatening enough damage to cause the naval commander to withdraw. Just before darkness, judging there was little more he could do to assist the battalion on the hill, he sailed his ships back to Palermo.

By this time, the American troops, pressed into a restricted defensive perimeter, were running out of ammunition. Fortunately, however, the Germans were paying little attention to them, for having pushed them into

a position where they could not interfere with the withdrawal, the Germans pulled out of the Naso ridge positions and came back through Brolo to their next delaying line.

The 3rd Division then moved forward, and at 7.30 am on 12th August a patrol made contact with the men on Monte Cipolla. Although they had lost 177 troops killed, wounded, and missing, they were still holding on.

Patton had come close to trapping a good part of Fries's division and perhaps even to rolling up the whole northern sector of Hube's front, but the battalion sent to make the landing had been too small to do the job. With more available seaborne transportation, with better air and naval support, Patton might have done some real damage to the German withdrawal.

Although Hube's Tortorici line was being pressed at the extreme flanks, he was hardly apprehensive, for his troops held extremely favourable positions on excellent defensive terrain that could be easily blocked by extensive use of mines and demolitions. Full-scale evacuation across the Strait of Messina started during the night of 11th August on schedule, and the only matter of concern to Hube was the need to hold Randazzo another day. Threatened by the 9th US and 78th British Divisions, Randazzo was a critical point, for it had to be held to permit the withdrawal of Rodt's 15th Panzer Grenadier Division and part of Conrath's Hermann Göring Division along a single exit.

During the first 13 days of August, Randazzo was struck by Allied aircraft making a total of 756 sorties – 425 medium bombers, 249 light bombers, and 72 fighter-bombers – but to no effect. The bombardments were nothing more than a nuisance and there was no break in the German timetable. On the night of 12th August when Hube withdrew his forces to the first of his three final phase lines, Rodt pulled his men out of Randazzo and made good his escape. American and British patrols entering on the morning of 13th August found

only a shattered, empty town.

Patton brought the 1st Division into the line again on 12th August. Despite the active offensive efforts of three American divisions – the 1st, 3rd, and 9th – Hube pulled back without trouble during the night of 14th August to his second phase line; by nightfall of 14th August only a single reinforced infantry battalion held the 29th Panzer Grenadier Division front.

Meanwhile, Conrath was fighting a leisurely battle of withdrawal, fending off the British with part of his Hermann Göring Division while sending the rest to Messina to cross the strait. On the evening of 13th August he gave up Taormina, 29 miles from Messina, and fell back to Hube's second phase line, and then, leaving a strong rearguard force, Conrath continued moving his division back to the ferrying points.

On 14th August the evacuation was going so well that Hube decided to extend the mass withdrawal by one night. Confident he could maintain an orderly retirement, he was determined to get as much equipment off the island as possible, and in order to maintain the timetable, he ordered the additional night inserted between the previously arranged third and fourth nights. Thus, the night of 16th August would still be known as the fifth night, although it would in actuality be the sixth and final period of the withdrawal.

On 15th August with Rodt's 15th Panzer Grenadier Division safely across the strait, the small forces remaining of the two other German divisions were largely out of contact with the Allied forces, now fighting the terrain and the demolitions rather than the enemy as they sought to advance. When Conrath and Fries reported that the Allies had regained contact late that day, Hube was satisfied that he could maintain the third phase line and get everyone off the island.

The ferry operations had started in earnest on the night of 11th August but the craft had run at full capacity for only a short time – from the onset of darkness until 8.45 pm, when they slowed and stopped temporarily because British Wellingtons bombed the strait and because some troops were

The bombing of Messina. A B-24 Liberator attacks the naval barracks and oil tanks

Part of Baade's defences in the Straits of Messina

slow in reaching the embarkation sites. Although the ferries carried less than capacity loads and made intermittent voyages during the rest of the night, the operation picked up in the morning of 12th August and throughout the day, at irregular intervals, the craft transported weapons and equipment across the water.

That night, when men again appeared north of Messina and waited patiently for the boats, a temporary failure in telephone communications between Messina and the mainland disrupted the operation and caused some confusion. Several ferries waited at an embarkation point for three hours, then departed shortly before the troops, who were late, finally arrived. At 2 am on 13th August, the ferries moved again. When Allied air attacks interfered with the movements in the narrow portion of the straits, Baade, despite Hube's original instructions, ferried troops across the strait during the daylight hours of 13th August. By that evening, he had

moved a total of 15,000 men, 1,300 vehicles, 21 tanks, and 22 assault guns to the mainland.

When the Germans on 13th August shifted to daylight operations for ferrying personnel, the Allied air force were committing 106 B-17s, 102 B-26s, 66 B-25s, and 135 P-38s in a huge raid near Rome – instead of concentrating these forces against the Messina strait area. The reason for the mainland air operation was, in the words of an air force headquarters report, 'the land battle (on Sicily) was going so well.'

The Italians were doing the best they could with their obsolete and limited equipment. Their train ferry caught fire on 12th August and was out of commission for 48 hours, but motor rafts, transporting men at the rate of 1,000 per trip, made a total of 20 voyages. Having repaired the train ferry and made it seaworthy, the Italians then loaded it with heavy artillery pieces, intending to tow the craft across the strait, but they were unable to find a tug, and eventually they scuttled the ferry to prevent the artillery from falling into Allied

ands.
Now Hube came to the rescue, and
Germans picked up Italian weapons
and equipment and moved them across
the strait in their ferries. Many pieces
were kept from the Allies, but most
were also lost to the Italians who never
saw the material again – the Germans
simply added the pieces to their own
stocks.

Alexander was unaware that the
evacuation had actually begun until
6th August when the British lost contact all along the front with the opposing troops who had slipped away.
On that day, he sent a radio message
to Tedder indicating his belief that
Germans and Italians were crossing
the straits in large numbers and sug-
gesting that the air forces mount a
strong effort against the movements.
But, already committed to striking
mainland targets in strength, Tedder
could only release some medium and
light bombers and some fighters and
fighter-bombers to pound the Messina
area. The pilots thus diverted from
mainland targets found their endea-
vours hampered; it was difficult to
penetrate the anti-aircraft defences,
and 'The immense concentration of
flak on both sides of the Narrows', a
pilot reported on the following day,
'makes it impossible to go down and
really search for targets thoroughly.'
The minor damage the Allied pilots
thus inflicted on embarkation and
disembarkation points, the Germans and
Italians quickly repaired.

On 15th August with air and naval
forts obviously impotent to deal
with the Axis withdrawal, the Allied
ground commanders attempted to do
something spectacular to cut the
movements. Three days earlier,
Patton had set in motion planning for
amphibious and airborne landings,
each on the scale of a regiment, each
to land well behind the German
defenders any time between 14th and
18th August. He designated a regimental combat team to train for the
amphibious venture, and after strenuous efforts, assembled enough shipping to transport it.

On the morning of 15th August as
3rd Division troops neared the turn
of the road leading to Messina 15
miles away, Patton telephoned Bradley and told him to land the regiment
designated for the seaborne landing.
He wanted the troops to come ashore
not at Bivio Salica as originally planned but at Spadafora, ten miles
farther east, but there could be no airborne operation as the 3rd Division
was already beyond the scheduled drop
zones near Barcellona. Now Patton's
principal motive was simply to speed
his advance into Messina ahead of
Montgomery.

Bradley told him that the amphibious operation would be useless. The
3rd Division was encountering only
light rearguard resistance and would
have troops waiting at Spadafora for
the amphibious force coming ashore,
but Patton insisted that the operation
was necessary, sending Keyes to
Truscott's command post to co-ordinate the naval and ground force
arrangements.

Unfortunately, owing to a fatal lack
of communication, the regiment was
put ashore at Bivio Salica in the
early hours of 16th August by which
time the 3rd Division was passing
through Spadafora, and by nightfall
its leading units approached the
Casazza crossroads near Messina and
the ridgeline overlooking the city. By
this time, too, Truscott had his long-
range artillery firing across the strait
into the Italian mainland; Bradley
had been right and the amphibious
operation useless.

Montgomery too had finally decided
to launch an amphibious operation,
perhaps spurred by Patton's efforts to
get to Messina before him. On 13th
August, Cunningham had asked Montgomery why he refused to make use
of what Cunningham called 'the price-
less asset of sea power' which would
give him 'flexibility of manoeuvre',
but Montgomery had seen no need for
so risky an enterprise. The campaign
was as good as over.

Two days later, however, he decided
otherwise. He now wanted a Com-
mando unit bolstered by tanks from the
British 4th Armoured Brigade to land
at Cape d'Ali on the morning of 16th
August, cut off the retreat of whatever
Germans remained, and speed into
Messina.

That evening, 15th August, Conrath's
rearguards moved out and headed for
Hube's third phase line, three miles
beyond Cape d'Ali, so the 400 British

troops who came ashore caught the tag end of the rearguard unit, which halted, turned, and stopped the amphibiously landed troops just north of Scaletta. After darkness on 16th August when Conrath's rearguards finally headed for Messina, the 400 troops moved forward, passing through Tremestieri, two miles south of Messina, at daybreak of 17th August, but there a demolished bridge across a deep ravine stopped their progress.

By then the Axis evacuation was about completed. Hube and Fries had left Sicily at 5.30 pm on 16th August and that night the last of the German rearguards departed – 200 men of the 29th Panzer Grenadier Division holding the Casazza crossroads four miles west of Messina, and the northern entrance into the city. Generale di Brigata Ettore Monacci, commander of the Italian army troops at Naval Base Messina, was the last high-ranking officer to leave the city, doing so after setting mines to demolish the port facilities.

At 6.35 am, 17th August, Hube reported to Kesselring that the evacuation operation had come to an end. An hour later, a German patrol boat picked up eight Italian soldiers paddling across the strait on a raft.

Several hours before midnight on 16th August a reinforced platoon of the 3rd Division pushed through the Casazza intersection and entered Messina, and early the following morning, other troops followed; there was no resistance.

At 7 am on the ridgeline overlooking Messina, Truscott received the city's civil dignitaries, who paid a ceremonial visit to the conquerors, and an hour later, Colonel Michele Tomasello appeared and offered to make a formal military surrender. Since Keyes had instructed Truscott to wait for Patton before entering Messina, Truscott sent his assistant division commander, Brigadier-General William Eagles, into the city with Tomasello to prepare the act of surrender, to supervise the American soldiers roving curiously through the streets, and, as Eagles later said, 'to see that the British did not capture the city from us after we had taken it.'

At 8.15 am the leader of the Commando troops halted at Tremestieri

by the destroyed bridge at the ravine decided to bypass the obstacle in jeep and race for Messina in an at tempt to get there before the Amer cans; but he reached Messina soon afte Eagles entered, made contact wit him, and learned to his dismay tha the Americans had taken the city.

At 10 am Patton arrived at the ridg line overlooking Messina. 'What i hell are you all standing around for' he shouted. Taking his place in a ca at the head of a motor cavalcade, b roared into Messina (accompanied a the way by enemy artillery fire com ing in from Baade's guns emplace across the straits), where he formall accepted the capitulation of Messin and by inference of Sicily, from

omasello.

By this time, the British armoured column that Montgomery had sent forward to link up with the Commandos had made contact with them, repaired the bridge, and headed into Messina. The tank crews and Commandos arrived just after the surrender ceremony, and the senior British officer walked over to Patton, shook hands, and said, 'It was a jolly good race. I congratulate you'.

Congratulations belonged, in fact, elsewhere.

The Germans had evacuated not quite 40,000 men of whom almost 4,500 were wounded; 9,600 vehicles; 94 guns; 47 tanks, 1,000 tons of ammunition; 970 tons of fuel; 15,700 tons of

The British 'bomb carpet' hides the pier at Messina

miscellaneous equipment, including much Italian material. The Italians, whose records were not quite so well kept, ferried somewhere between 70,000 and 75,000 troops across; around 500 vehicles; between 75 and 100 artillery pieces; and 12 mules.

Thus, after 38 days of struggle, ended the Sicily campaign – on a note of glee for both sides. But the triumphant Allied entry into Messina seemed shrill and somewhat empty beside the achievement of the Axis withdrawal of almost 125,000 men from the island.

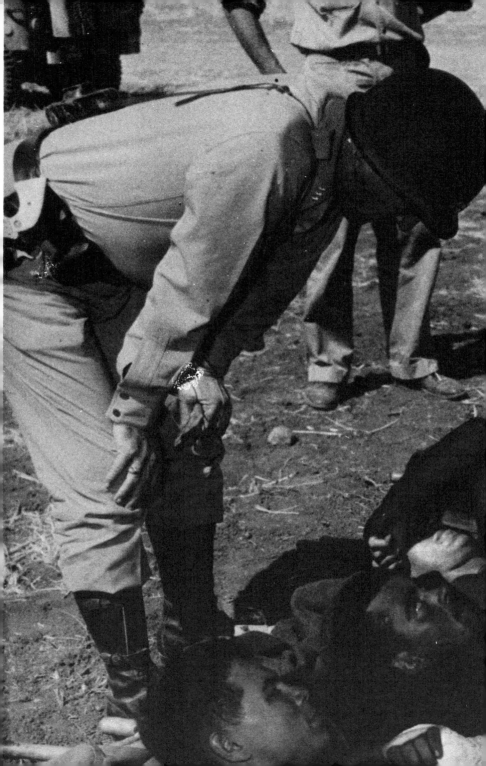

The slapping incident

The most controversial subject to emerge from the Sicily campaign was the so-called slapping incident involving Patton. A flamboyant yet thoroughly professional soldier, Patton had, as a result of the Sicily operations, captured the fancy of the troops and of the American public. His verve and colour, together with his unquestionable military competence and proficiency in battle, had already made him a legendary figure and put him in the forefront of the American combat leaders. Yet his slapping of two soldiers whom he suspected of malingering almost destroyed his reputation and his future effectiveness in the war. There were actually two incidents.

The first occurred on 3rd August near Nicosia. Accompanied by Major-General John Lucas (a War Department observer dispatched by Marshall to act as his eyes and ears in the Mediterranean theatre), and escorted by the hospital commander and other medical officers, Patton entered the receiving tent of the 15th Evacuation Hospital. He spoke to the wounded men in the tent who were awaiting treatment, and he was deeply touched by their courage and forbearance. He commended each man in an emotional manner and seemed several times on the verge of tears.

Then he came upon a soldier who had just arrived in the hospital, who had no bandage, no mark of a wound, but who sat in dazed hopelessness and depression. A doctor at the clearing station just behind the front who had sent him to the hospital had made a preliminary diagnosis of 'psychoneurosis anxiety; state - moderate severe'.

Patton read the medical tag attached to the soldier, than asked him what the matter was.

'I guess I can't take it,' he replied.

Patton flew into a rage. Cursing the soldier in his high-pitched, squealing voice, he slapped the man across the face with his gloves, and finally grabbed him and threw him out of the tent.

Calming somewhat, Patton then concluded his inspection of the hospi-

Previous page: **Patton inspects the wounded, wearing his pearl-handled Colt revolver**

tal, went on to tour a portion of the front, and returned to his head quarters, where he had a memoran dum prepared for distribution to hi senior commanders. 'It has come t my attention', he wrote, 'that a ver small number of soldiers are going t the hospital on the pretext that the are nervously incapable of comba Such men are cowards, and bring dis credit on the Army and disgrace t their comrades... You will take meas ures to see that such cases are no sent to the hospital, but are deal with in their units. Those who are no willing to fight will be tried by Court Martial for cowardice in the face o the enemy.'

Patton believed that he had don the man a service. In his diary h noted: 'I gave him the devil, slappe his face with my gloves and kicke him out of the hospital . . . One some times slaps a baby to bring it to.'

At the hospital, a corpsman ha picked up the soldier and had taker him to a ward tent. Here he was foun to be running a high fever and had a history of chronic diarrhea, and tw day later, doctors made a final diag nosis of his case, finding chronic dysentery and malaria; on 9th Augus they shipped him to North Africa fo extended treatment.

A day later, on 10th August, Patton dropped in unexpectedly at the 93r Evacuation Hospital. A medical office met him and escorted him to the receiving tent, where 15 patient had just arrived from the front an were sitting or lying on cots awaiting to be seen by a doctor.

Again, Patton started down the lin of cots, speaking with each man. He asked where the soldier was hurt an how he had been wounded or injured and at each response he was visibly affected, and he commended each fo his bravery and endurance.

Seated on the fourth cot was an artilleryman who was trembling violently.

Patton asked him what the trouble was.

'It's my nerves,' he said and began to sob.

Patton was furious. 'What did yo say?' he shouted.

'It's my nerves,' the soldier repeated 'I can hear the shells come over,' he

plained, still crying, 'but I can't bear them burst.'

Patton turned to the medical officer. 'What's this man talking about?' he asked. 'What's wrong with him, if anything?'

The medical officer reached for the soldier's tag to read the diagnosis.

Before the medical officer could answer, Patton began to yell. 'Your nerves, hell. You are just a goddamned coward, you yellow son of a bitch. You're a disgrace to the Army and you're going right back to the front to fight, although that's too good for you. You ought to be lined up against a wall and shot. In fact, I ought to shoot you myself right now, God damn you.'

He reached for his pistol, pulled it from his holster, and waved it in the soldier's face.

The young man sat quivering on his cot.

Patton struck him sharply across the face with his free hand, continuing to yell and curse, but by this time, the commander of the hospital had entered the receiving tent.

Seeing him, Patton shouted, 'I want you to get that man out of here right away. I won't have these other brave boys seeing such a bastard babied.'

Putting his pistol back in his holster, Patton started to leave the tent. Then he turned suddenly and saw the soldier sobbing uncontrollably, he rushed back and slapped him across the face, this time with such force that he knocked the man's helmet liner off his head and sent it rolling out of the tent.

At this, the hospital commander placed himself between Patton and the soldier.

Patton strode out of the tent.

The hospital commander followed him.

Outside the tent, Patton said to the medical officer who commanded the hospital, 'I meant what I said about getting that coward out of here. I won't have those cowardly bastards hanging around our hospitals. We'll probably have to shoot them some-time anyway, or we'll raise a breed of moron.'

Some time later, the hospital psychiatrist confirmed the prelimi-nary diagnosis made at the clearing station: severe shell shock.

Patton casually mentioned the incident in a conversation with Bradley, who paid little attention to it, but meanwhile the medical officer in charge of the hospital had written a full account of what had happened, submitting it to the II Corps Surgeon. He protested not only Patton's be-haviour but his interference with medical procedures.

The corps Surgeon carried the report to Bradley's chief of staff, who rushed it to Bradley's office. Bradley read the report, then told his chief of staff to lock it in a safe and do no-thing more – and clearly, there was no-thing further Bradley could have done, for submitting the report up the chain of command would have meant sending it to Patton. The only alter-native for Bradley was to bypass his immediate superior, Patton, and send the report directly to Eisenhower, but this would have been a breach of military loyalty.

By this time, however, news of the occurrences had spread among most of the American troops in Sicily. Be-cause it was common knowledge, three American war correspondents heard the story and discussed it among themselves, but none of the three would file the story for publication, for all realized the impact it would have on the public, on Patton's career, and on his future usefulness to the war effort.

Eisenhower learned of both inci-dents through medical channels. His own surgeon gave him a detailed report on 16th August, the day before the campaign ended, and despite the shock this gave Eisenhower, he decided to give Patton a chance to explain. On the following day, Eisen-hower wrote Patton a personal letter offering to let him deny the allega-tions; but he warned that if the allega-tions were correct in any part, Patton would have to be severely censured. He sent the letter to be delivered personally by a general officer.

'I am well aware,' Eisenhower had written, 'of the necessity for hardness and toughness on the battlefield. I clearly understand that firm and drastic measures are at times neces-sary in order to secure desired objec-tives. But this does not excuse bru-

tality, abuse of the sick, nor exhibi-
tion of uncontrollable temper in
front of subordinates . . . if there is a
very considerable element of truth in
the allegations accompanying this
letter, I must so seriously question
your good judgment and your self-
discipline as to raise serious doubts in
my mind as to your future usefulness.'

If any part of the story was true,
Patton was, Eisenhower said, to make
amends, 'apology or otherwise', to
the individuals concerned.

Completely chastened, Patton was
agreeable to doing everything that
Eisenhower considered necessary, and
he set about to make amends. He
talked with the two soldiers involved,
explained his motives, and apologized.
'In each case,' he later wrote to
Eisenhower, 'I stated I should like to
shake hands with them, and in each
case they accepted my offer.'

Then he talked with the medical
personnel who had been present and
he expressed regret for 'my impulsive
actions.' And finally, he addressed all
the divisions in the Seventh Army,
speaking to each in turn, and apologized 'for any occasions when I may
have harshly criticized individuals.'

His reply, sent to Eisenhower on
29th August, assured the Supreme
Allied Commander that Patton had
had no intention of 'being either harsh
or cruel in my treatment of the two
soldiers in question. My sole purpose
was to try and restore in them a just
appreciation of their obligation as
men and as soldiers.' He recalled an
incident during World War I, when a
close friend had lost his nerve 'in an
exactly analogous manner,' and this
officer had suffered years of mental
anguish before finally committing
suicide. 'Both my friend and the medical men with whom I discussed his
case assured me that had he been
roundly checked at the time of his
first misbehaviour, he would have been
restored to a normal state'. That was
why he had done what he had, and 'I
felt I had probably saved an immortal
soul.'

Satisfied by Patton's explanation
and activities, Eisenhower called in
a group of reporters who had heard the
story and informed them of Patton's
apology. He said he had decided to
keep Patton rather than dismiss him,

for he was too valuable an asset in th
fighting war, and the corresponden
were sympathetic and declined to fi
stories on the slappings.

This might have been the end of th

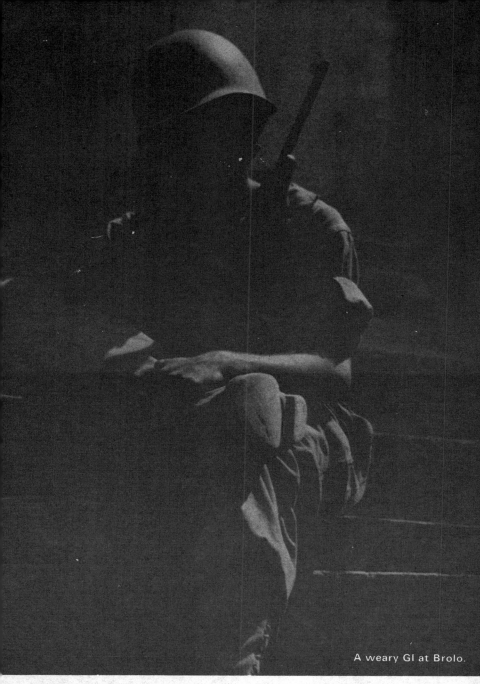

A weary GI at Brolo.

incident had not a reporter who came from the United States to the theatre in November heard the story. He released it over the radio. Despite the public uproar that followed, Eisenhower refused to change his decision.

Patton's leadership in combat during the European campaigns of 1944 and 1945 more than justified Eisenhower's course of action.

Victory

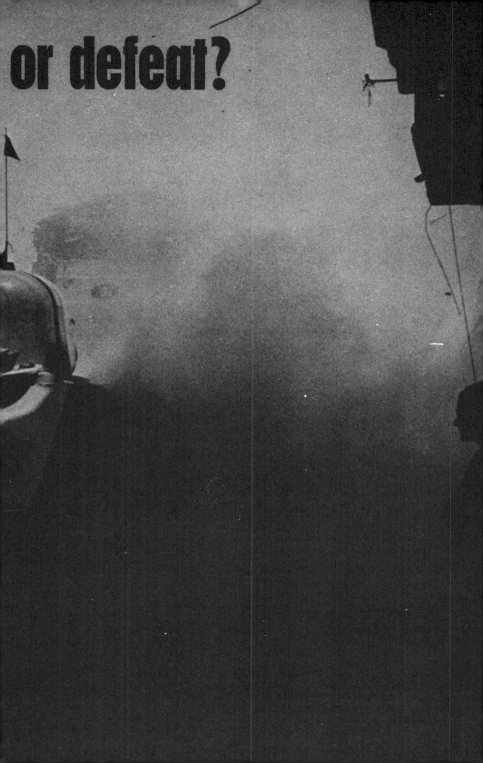

or defeat?

The controversy over Patton and the slappings has obscured a broader and more important question: who won the battle of Sicily?

The Allies, obviously. They accomplished what they set out to do – conquer the island. In the process, they provided greater security for their shipping in the Mediterranean, gained airfields closer to primary bombing targets in Germany, cracked the Italo-German alliance, greased the skids for Mussolini's slide to obscurity, brought the Italians close to capitulation, and, by their successful execution of the terribly complicated aspects of amphibious landings, served notice on the Germans of what would become an inexorable march to victory.

Moreover, the American ground forces reached maturity and gained prestige equal to the British, while Patton rose to prominence as America's counterpart to Montgomery. Bradley demonstrated his continued competence, as did such division commanders as Truscott, Middleton, and Eddy, all of whom would go on to more significant responsibilities. Simonds would later command a corps, and Dempsey and Leese would go on from corps command to head British armies, one in northwest Europe, the other in Italy.

Eisenhower again showed his grasp of and control over the ramifications of high Allied command, and so too did Alexander, who always had a remarkably stimulating effect on British soldiers and whose loose-reined leadership had worked as well in Sicily as in Tunisia. 'At times,' Eisenhower once wrote, 'it seems that he (Alexander) alters his own plans and ideas merely to meet an objection or a suggestion of a subordinate, so as to avoid direct command methods' – but like Eisenhower, Alexander cemented the Anglo-American coalition, and his skill in handling two most difficult subordinates – Montgomery and Patton – was an achievement of first rank.

As a result of the triumph in Sicily, Eisenhower made his final decision on 16th August with respect to post-Sicily operations. He would send the Eighth Army across the Strait of Messina to invade the toe of Italy as soon as possible, probably around 1st September and he would dispatch a new and untried US Fifth Army to invade the Salerno beaches on 9th September. Whether or not this was a sound decision is beyond the scope of this book.

But what of Allied tactics during the Battle for Sicily? The whole Allied plan had been governed by the anticipation of strenuous resistance, and thus was one of caution and conservatism. The Allies had avoided gamble and risk, playing it safe; and in the final analysis they made a power drive – a frontal assault that was inexcusable in the rugged ground of Sicily.

Certainly the supremacy of Allied air and naval forces could have been better utilized for massive outflanking operations to trap the Axis forces – and most damning of all, no joint plan was drawn to prevent the Axis evacuation. To some extent this derived from the separation of the senior commanders – Eisenhower was in Algiers, Cunningham was at Malta, Tedder was near Tunis, and Alexander at Cassibile; to some extent, it followed a preoccupation with what was to happen beyond Sicily, a concentration on anticipated strategic action rather than on the business at hand, the ruthless extermination of the adversary.

The Allies nevertheless inflicted considerable losses on the Axis forces. The German casualties in dead and captured totalled about 12,000, and an estimated 145,000 Italians were killed or captured.

In contrast, the Allies lost less than 20,000 men – about 7,500 Americans, 11,500 British, and they captured about 120,000 prisoners, sending about 80,000 to North Africa, and granting island paroles to the rest.

From these figures of captured and evacuated, plus an estimated 20,000 others who were ferried to the mainland during the campaign because of wounds or other reasons, it is reasonable to assume that there were approximately 250,000 Axis troops in Sicily at peak strength – 200,000 Italians, 50,000 Germans. These had stood off two Allied armies – the Seventh with a peak strength of about 200,000 men, the Eighth with a strength of 250,000.

Counting Allied combat strength as one-third of total strength – the rest

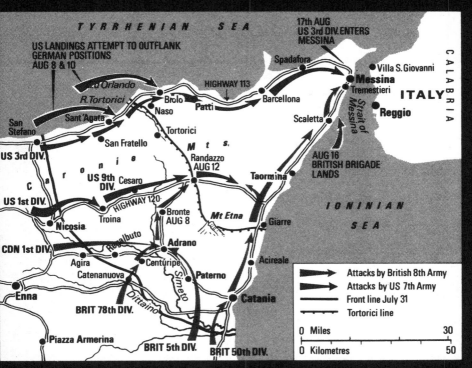

The final stages: convergence on Messina

Above: An Italian tends an exhausted soldier. The local police were retained by the Allies in captured towns. *Right:* A German prisoner has his papers read

being support and logistical troops – the Allies had fought with 150,000 men, three times as many as the Germans, and if the Italian troops, as was sometimes said, were more a hindrance than a help, the Allies should have overpowered the Germans far more expeditiously. That they were unable to do so might be explained by two observations – the Axis troops were eminently skilful in the defensive use of the rugged terrain of Sicily; and the Italian troops, despite their antiquated equipment and the rotten political and military system that deprived them consistently of the material and spiritual sustenance of combat, were far more battleworthy than was usually accorded them.

Given the deteriorating Italo-German alliance and the decision almost at the beginning of the Sicily campaign to abandon the island ultimately, the German and Italian troops won a moral victory. Fighting a gigantic delaying action, a handful of ground troops, without naval support and with only intermittent and relatively weak air assistance, kept two Allied armies at bay.

That they fought to uphold a noxious tyranny that all men of good will condemn, must not obscure their valiant and skilful military achievement.

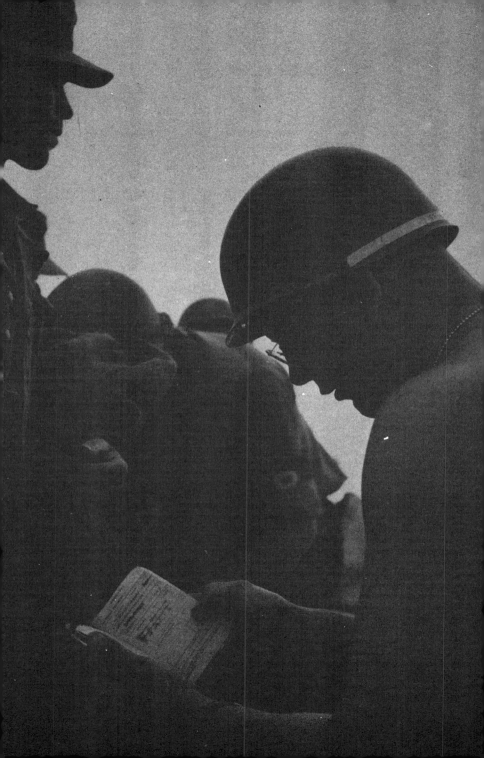

Bibliography

A Soldier's Story General Omar N Bradley (Eyre & Spottiswoode, London. Holt, New York)
Command Missions General Lucian K Truscott (Dutton, New York)
War As I Knew It General George S Patton, Jr (Houghton Mifflin, Boston)
Strategic Planning for Coalition Warfare, 1943-1944 Maurice Matloff (Govt Printing Office, Washington)
Soldier To the Last Day Albert Kesselring (William Kimber, London) (US title: *A Soldier's Record* (Morrow, New York)
Sicily: The Assault David Woodward (History of the Second World War, Purnell, London)
Sicily: The Conquest Peter Kemp (History of the Second World War, Purnell, London)
The Fall of Mussolini Anthony Rhodes (History of the Second World War, Purnell, London)
By Air to Battle: The Official Account of the British 1st and 6th Airborne Divisions (HMSO, London)
Ciano's Diary ed Malcolm Muggeridge (Heinemann, London. Doubleday, New York)
Crusade in Europe Dwight D Eisenhower (Heinemann, London. Doubleday, New York)
Benito Mussolini Christopher Hibbert (Longmans, London. Little Brown & Co., Boston)
A Don at War David Hunt (William Kimber, London)
A Sailor's Odyssey Admiral Lord Cunningham (Hutchinson, London. Dutton, New York)
Sicily and the Surrender of Italy A N Garland and H M Smyth (Government Printing Officer, Washington)
The Campaign in Italy Eric Linklater (HMSO London)
El Alamein to the River Sangro Field-Marshal Montgomery of Alamein (Hutchinson, London. Dutton, New York)
Eight Years Overseas Field-Marshal Sir Henry Maitland Wilson (Hutchinson, London)
Memoirs Field-Marshal Montgomery of Alamein (Collins, London. World, New York)
The Rome-Berlin Axis Elizabeth Wiskemann (Oxford University Press, Oxford and New York)